WITNESSES TO THE HOLY MASS

AND OTHER SERMONS

WITNESSES TO THE HOLY MASS
AND OTHER SERMONS

Sermons preached at Tyburn
during a Solemn Triduum in honor of
the English Martyrs
May 1-4, 1904,
and
at York on the occasion of the Ransom Pilgrimage,
May 28, 1901

By the Rev.
DOM BEDE CAMM, O.S.B.
of Erdington Abbey

Requiem Press
Columbia, SC
2004

Witnesses to the Holy Mass was originally published by Art and Book Company, England 1904 under the title: *Tyburn and the English Martyrs*. This 2004 edition has new typesetting and includes new footnotes, minor editorial revisions and corrections to the text.

Jacket Art by Elizabeth Nyikos

Requiem Press
P.O. Box 210155
Columbia, SC 29221-0155
1-888-708-7675

Nihil Obstat: Ansgar, Abbot of Erdington
Imprimatur: Edward, Bishop of Birmingham
June 11, 1904

(Publishers Note: the Nihil Obstat and Imprimatur apply only to the original text and not to the preface or the new footnotes.)

ISBN 0-9758542-0-8

Printed in the United States of America

Contents

Publishers Note: The biblical quotations found herein are from and follow the enumeration of the Douay-Rheims edition of the Old and New Testaments.

Publisher's Preface

*"And fear ye not them that kill the body, and are not able to kill
the soul: but rather fear him that can destroy both soul and
body in hell."* Matt. 10: 28

It is often spoken of: fifty years ago in America the Catholic Church was strong, orthodox, and faithful. Yet within a few decades we have become a Catholic population ignorant of the doctrines of the Holy Catholic Faith; we have (some) shepherds who fail to teach or uphold the Truth and scandalize the faithful with their passive allowance of abuse and disregard Christ's Vicar; we hear that less than 50% of Catholics believe in the Real Presence; we hear of many other things inconceivable just 50 years ago. How did this happen in so few years?

"Who would have guessed that a period of peace and sunshine was so suddenly to be changed into one of tempest and gloom? And yet we now see clearly enough that there were ominous signs of the coming change, had men only looked for them, long before the storm finally broke. The land seemed full of beautiful fruits and flowers, but there was a blight in the air, a canker in the heart of it all. And this blight, this canker, was the prevailing worldliness of the time. All this material prosperity had had a corrupting effect on those to whose pastoral care the flock of Christ

had been committed; ... the bishops were in many cases rather statesmen and politicians than ministers of Christ."
- Dom Bede Camm -

In early 16th century England, the Catholic Church was the pride of all Europe. The Protestant Revolt had not yet approached Britain's shores. The King was "Defender of the Church". Yet, in just a few years there commenced a century of martyrdom and persecution of Catholic faithful. Many, many fell away from the Faith of their fathers – among them, many bishops and priests. The Holy Sacrifice of the Mass was outlawed and obedience to Christ's vicar and the doctrines of the Church dismissed. The persecution was fearsome and violent.

Dom Bede Camm's words quoted above refer to 16th century England before the storm broke; they could equally refer to the mid-20th century in America. But there is a difference.

We have no gallows from which to hang in the present age. No one is being drawn towards the butcher's block. Our faithfulness is not proven in blood. Our fate is worse than those of days of old. Our bodies are intact, but our souls and the souls of our children are being taken and destroyed. And this is Christ's concern for us in the words at the head of this preface.

Six sermons preached 100 years ago across the ocean; sermons commemorating martyrs of the Holy Catholic Church whose blood was shed across the oceans and across the centuries; six sermons preached by a convert to the Faith, a Benedictine monk, whose purpose was to inspire and to pray for the (re)conversion of England to the Faith of her fathers. But this prayer for England should also be a prayer for the conversion of our own country. The martyrs' tales herein do not just belong to England, but to the whole Church.

The Holy Sacrifice of the Altar is not outlawed in America, but is profaned by the lukewarmness of the souls in the congregation. We need to renew our devotion to the Holy Eucharist. We need to pray for the conversion of souls. We need to mortify and persecute our own bodies for the sake of the conversion of the souls of our brethren and of our children. If the Destroyer is not persecuting our bodies – he is certainly pursuing our souls with the temptations of worldliness and lukewarmness.

This is why Requiem Press has determined to reprint this volume. The sermons which follow will help us see the priority that our fathers placed on the Faith and the sacraments - a priority that is often absent in our hearts today. These will inspire us to greater devotion to the Holy Mass; greater love for the doctrines of the Church ("*on His law he shall meditate day and night*" Ps. 1:2) taught by Christ's vicar.

By the reading of these tales of martyrs and the contemplation of their sacrifices, may we be inspired anew and our flames of love be rekindled so that we may fervently pray that God raise up saints among us once more!

Oremus pro invicem! – Let us pray for each other!

The Publisher

His hurdle draws us with him to the Cross,
His speeches there provoke us for to die,
His death doth say this life is but a loss,
His martyred blood from heaven to us doth cry,
His first and last and all conspire in this
To show the way that leadeth us to bliss

Blessed be God which lent him so much grace,
Thanked be Christ which blessed His martyr so,
Happy is he which sees his Master's face;
Cursed all they that thought to work him woe;
Bounden be we to give eternal praise
To Jesus' name which such a man did raise.

From a Poem on St. Edmund Campion, S.J.
By St. Henry Walpole, S.J.

INTRODUCTION

THESE pages contain the substance of the sermons preached in the Convent Chapel at Tyburn on the feast of the English Martyrs and the triduum which preceded it, in May, 1904. They were not preached from manuscript, with one exception, but have been written out since with the help of shorthand notes which were taken down during their delivery.

I am but too conscious that they are unworthy of being preserved in a permanent form, and it is with reluctance that I have yielded to the desire of the Reverend Mother and community to have them printed. But it was represented to me that they might help to spread devotion to the martyrs, and at the same time to draw attention to the sanctuary now raised at Tyburn, and to the pilgrimage of which it is the centre.

Those who love the martyrs (and what Catholic worthy of the name can help loving them?) must indeed thank God that now there is an altar raised upon this sacred spot where the Holy Sacrifice of the Mass is continually pleaded for the conversion of our country, and the incense of intercession goes up day and night from fervent hearts before our divine Lord, exposed on His Eucharistic throne.

More than three hundred years ago this was foretold, and it has now been accomplished in our own day. Truly it is the Lord's doing, and it is marvelous in our eyes!

It is true that there is yet much to be done. We must not be content until there rises on this spot a votive church, worthy of those who here shed their blood for Christ. As Paris has her noble Chapelle Expiatoire in memory of the illustrious victims of the Revolution, so London must have her martyrs' shrine, resplendent with the beauty of holiness, where her children may gather together to praise Him who is wonderful in His saints.

He will no doubt inspire some generous hearts to raise a monument of expiation, which by its material beauty will draw to Tyburn multitudes of those to whom His martyrs are as yet unknown, and thus exert a powerful influence in the great work of the conversion of England. Hither, too, will flock pilgrims ever more numerous and more fervent, praising God for His mercies, and imploring the grace of conversion for their separated brethren.

This work indeed is already begun. The little chapel in which these sermons were preached was too small to hold the pilgrims who were drawn there, and there are already hundreds who have gladly seized the privilege of inscribing the names of those in whose conversion they are interested in the book which lies ever before the Blessed Sacrament at Tyburn.

Soon, no doubt, public processions of pilgrims will pass down Oxford Street and Edgware Road to this little sanctuary, just as they now do to the Tyburn at York each Whitsuntide. Hither will come converts to give thanks to God and His martyrs for the priceless gift of faith; hither, too, will come the representatives of those grand old English families who remained faithful through the long dark years of persecution, and who gladly gave their sons to die for Christ at Tyburn. Hither will come those candid, generous souls who, brought up in error, are struggling to be free. And all will here invoke the glorious martyrs who dyed with their blood this sacred soil.

And now let me add a word about the site of Tyburn.

The place takes its name from the little stream of Tybourne, or Tyburn. It consisted, we are told, of two branches, one of which crossed Oxford Street near Stratford Place, while the other, further west, followed nearly the course of the present Westbourne Terrace and the Serpentine. Five hundred years ago it was a pleasant brook with rows of elms growing on its banks. These trees became the originals of the "Tyburn Tree." They were used for executions, and on one of them Roger Mortimer, the murderer of Edward II, is said to have been hung.

Later on the place of execution was moved further east, to the corner of the Edgware Road and the Oxford Road, where it became a fixture for centuries.

The triangular gibbet was a permanent erection. A new one was erected for the martyrdom of Blessed John Storey (June 1, 1571). We are told that Blessed Edmund Campion[1], who had been present at the aged martyr's trial, would often make pilgrimages to it while he was still free, and would walk between its posts with bare head and with a profound bow, in honor both of the cross which it figured and of the martyrs whose blood had consecrated it, and also because, as he told Father Robert Persons, he knew that it was one day to be the place of his own conflict.

A piece of the old gibbet was kept as a sacred relic in the English College at Valladolid at the beginning of the seventeenth century. The exact spot where the gallows stood is probably to be identified with the site of the house at the southeast corner of Connaught Place, for in the lease granted by the Bishop of London, to whom the property belonged, this fact is particularly mentioned. Quantities of human bones were found when Connaught Place was built. The gibbet stood on a small eminence. Tyburn tollhouse (which was removed in 1829) subsequently stood on the spot. A gate crossed the road, and the site of this is still marked by a stone with the inscription, "Here stood Tyburn Gate," which is placed against the park railings, almost opposite the site of the gallows.

In an old plan of London, dated 1708, Oxford Street is called "Tyburn Road." It is described as lying "between St. Giles' Pound, east, and the lane leading to the gallows, west."

Tyburn Convent does not therefore appear to occupy the exact site of the gallows. But it is not many yards distant from the spot, and it doubtless stands on ground which has been soaked with the blood of martyrs, and in which their sacred relics may be still buried.

---

[1] Edmund Campion was canonized a saint on 25 October 1970 by Pope Paul VI as one of the 40 English and Welsh martyrs.

Tyburn was a place of pilgrimage even during the days of persecution. As we have seen, the Blessed Edmund Campion himself inaugurated this pilgrimage, just as the venerable Margaret Clitheroe began that to the York Tyburn.[2] An illustrious pilgrim came here on an occasion which has become historical. Queen Henrietta Maria[3], soon after her arrival in London, went there to pray beneath the gibbet. This so incensed the Protestants that it became the cause of the King's sending her ladies back to France.

The event was greatly exaggerated by the popular outcry , and it was pretended that the Queen had been forced by her spiritual directors to walk barefoot from her palace to the gallows.

The example thus set by one of the martyrs of Tyburn, and imitated by a Queen of England and a daughter of France, has never been wholly forgotten by the Catholics of London. We read in the life of the saintly Mother Margaret Hallahan, O.S.D., that as a child (she was born in 1803) "she used to accompany other pious Catholics in the visits which it was then customary among them to pay to Tyburn in memory of the martyrs who had suffered there since the Reformation. These pilgrimages were performed with great devotion, and generally on Sundays, but their object was kept carefully concealed from Protestant neighbors."

No doubt the removal of the gibbet (the place of execution was changed to Newgate in 1783) and the building of houses on the sacred site tended to put a stop to these pious pilgrimages. They may now, thank God, be resumed under happier auspices.

The devoted religious who have made their home at Tyburn devote themselves to prayer for the conversion of our country. Two large wax tapers burn continually before the Blessed Sacrament, one for the King and the other for England. Beneath the chapel, where the Blessed Sacrament is perpetually exposed,

---

[2] Margaret Clitheroe (Clitherow) was canonized a saint on 25 October 1970 by Pope Paul VI as one of the 40 English and Welsh Martyrs.

[3] Queen Henrietta Marie (1609-1669) of France was married to King Charles I of England. While King Charles valued her advice greatly in later years, she was always looked on with suspicion by others because she was Catholic.

is an oratory dedicated to the blessed martyrs, and enriched with their pictures and their relics. It is to be hoped that these will in time be greatly increased, for there is no resting place so fitting for relics of the martyrs as this shrine; and when in God's good time a permanent chapel replaces the present temporary one, its walls will, it is hoped, be adorned with frescoes representing the martyrs offering their hearts to the Sacred Heart of their Lord.

God has already shown by such manifest signs that this work at Tyburn is His own work, that we cannot but believe with fullest confidence that it is destined greatly to develop and to become a permanent source of blessings for the Church in England. May He in His mercy grant that through the labors and prayers of the nuns of Tyburn the glory of His martyrs may be greatly increased and the conversion of England hastened.

If the publication of these sermons does anything, however small, towards the accomplishment of this great work, the writer will indeed be rewarded beyond his deserts. He would, in conclusion, venture to beg the prayers of those who read his words for several intentions of great importance to himself and to others.

"Jesus, convert England; Jesus, have mercy on this country."

D. B. C.

Erdington Abbey, Birmingham.
Feast of the Sacred Heart, June 10, 1904.

I

The Martyrs
the Consolation of the Heart of God

Sunday, May 1, 1904

*"In servis suis consolabitur Deus. — God shall
find His consolation in His servants."*

WHAT a wonderful thought it is, dear brethren in Jesus
Christ: how consoling and inspiring, that the great God who has
all things and can do all things, whose bliss from all eternity has
known no limits and no imperfections, should nevertheless desire
our love, should yearn after it with unspeakable longing, should
seek it with unwearied patience, and, having obtained it, should
rejoice over it as a treasure of great price! "My son, give Me thy
heart," He cries to each one of us, and to those who respond to the
call, to them He reveals all the hidden secrets of His heart, on
them He pours out the riches of His love, in them He finds His
consolation and His joy.

Our divine Lord asks for faithful friends, for friends who
will be true till death, who will not shrink from trials and sufferings
for His sake, who will embrace the cross with joy because it unites
them more closely to Him, who will welcome persecution, torture
— yes, and death itself — in order to prove more surely the reality
and constancy of their devotion.

Our Lord does not seek for mere fair weather friends. It is
very easy to think we love Him when all things are bright around
us, easy to have hot feelings in prayer, to delight in beautiful
services, music and ceremonial, easy to fancy we are very devout,
as long as there is nothing serious to give up for God's love, no

fierce struggles with the world and the devil, no wearing conflict with the flesh. But it is temptation, it is sacrifice which proves and tests our love, it is the day of darkness and gloom which reveals the true nature of our devotion, and happy indeed are they who in the hour of trial are found faithful, even unto death, for they are those blessed ones who console the heart of God.

There never, perhaps, was a time when all things seemed brighter than in the early days of Henry VIII. Never had the Church seemed more flourishing, more prosperous, more honored. The beauty and riches of the churches were the wonder of Christendom, and foreign visitors to England were amazed at their magnificence. Stately monasteries and religious houses covered the land, and for the most part were filled with men and women who had given up the world for Christ, and whose lives of unostentatious beneficence made them beloved of the people around their gates. The bishops and higher clergy were learned and munificent, and foreign scholars, like the famous Erasmus, found in them their most generous patrons. A new life was transforming the ancient universities, where the study of Greek was eagerly pursued under the auspices of men like Colet and Fisher. The German heresiarchs, who were beginning their revolt against the Church and her teaching, found their most strenuous and formidable opponents in England, where the Lord High Chancellor of the realm — nay, the very monarch himself — did not disdain to break a lance with them on behalf of the orthodox faith. The king was the most brilliant, the most generous, the most devout in Christendom. He was wont to hear four or five Masses a day; he went on pilgrimage to the shrine of our Lady of Walsingham, walking the last few miles barefoot; he wrote treatises on theological subjects, such as the necessity of vocal prayer, and indeed until his elder brother's death had intended to take holy orders. Above all he was the most strenuous supporter of the claims of the Holy See to be found in all his realms. When all was thus smiling who could have foreseen the storm?

Who would have guessed that a period of peace and sunshine was so suddenly to be changed into one of tempest and gloom?

And yet we now see clearly enough that there were ominous signs of the coming change, had men only looked for them, long before the storm finally broke. The land seemed full of beautiful fruits and flowers, but there was a blight in the air, a canker in the heart of it all. And this blight, this canker, was the prevailing worldliness of the time. All this material prosperity had had a corrupting effect on those to whose pastoral care the flock of Christ had been committed; the riches of the monastic orders had too often become a snare and a hindrance to regular observance; the bishops were in many cases rather statesmen and politicians than ministers of Christ. And, what was even worse, there was a strong undercurrent of what are known as Gallican ideas, a fatal consequence of the disedifying spectacle presented to Christendom by the great schism, and the various scandals to which it had given rise.[4]

And so, when the storm burst and God looked down upon this land of ours to seek servants and friends after His own heart, he found so few, so very few. A little cloud, no bigger than a man's hand at first, had risen in the sky, and before men were aware of it, it had overshadowed the heavens from one end to another, and as the lightning flashed and the thunder rolled, the shepherds cowered trembling before the fury of the storm, and too often fled, leaving their flocks to perish. Yet even here, God found His consolation in His faithful servants.

Thus, when the Duke of Norfolk warned the Blessed Thomas More that the anger of the king was death (Indignatio principis mors est), the blessed martyr calmly replied: "Then the only difference between you and me, my lord, is that I must die today and you tomorrow."[5]

I need not say much as to the causes of the fierce persecution which now broke upon England. You all know that it

---

[4] "Gallican ideas" refer to certain opinions peculiar to the Church in France in the late 17th century which generally favor limiting the pope's authority in favor of the local bishops and the temporal rulers. However the pope's primacy was never questioned.

[5] Thomas More was canonized a saint on 19 May 1935.

was directly due to the evil passions of the king. He fell into sin and desired a woman who was not his wife, and tried by every means to induce the Pope to grant him his unlawful desire. When he found that both threats and cajolery were powerless to obtain from the Holy See a license for bigamy, he determined to make himself Pope and drag the country with him into heresy and schism. Henry's dominant passions were obstinacy and self-will, and these fatal passions hurried him along the downward path, for he was too proud ever to own himself in the wrong, or to retrace the steps once taken. He had threatened the Pope that if he would not yield to his wishes he would set up a schismatic church, and he was determined to keep his word, though he fully knew the heinousness of such a crime. And he pursued his course to the bitter end, though he had to shed rivers of blood — the best and purest blood in England — before he could consummate his apostasy. Unhappily he had at his side a minister, Thomas Cromwell, whose avowed aim was to satisfy in all things his master's desires whether lawful or not. This man's Machiavellian policy was but too faithfully imitated by the apostate archbishop, Thomas Cranmer, a man who had been raised to the chair of St. Augustine in order to assist the king in his evil work, and who never shrank from any infamy at his master's bidding. And thus the hour of trial came on England, and alas! for the most part, found her unprepared.

In the spring of 1534 the parliament, clergy and people were called upon to take an oath by which they acknowledged the validity of the king's marriage with Anne Boleyn, and repudiated his former marriage as unlawful. This, indirectly at least, aimed at the authority of the Roman pontiff, for it denied his right to interfere in the matter, and he had just pronounced against the king's second marriage and commanded him to return to his lawful wife. Nevertheless, the great majority of clergy and people were so cowed by the Tudor tyranny, so terrified by the frightful vengeance taken on those who dared to withstand the royal will, that they yielded and took the oath. Most of them thought, no doubt, that this was but a passing storm, and that when the king's passion for Anne Boleyn had been satisfied he would be reconciled once more to the Holy See and to his outraged wife; and that in the meantime they could thus preserve their property and their lives.

And so, my brethren, when God sought for faithful friends, He found but few. Yet, thank God, there were some, some to console His heart. Some there were who only longed to share the cross of their Lord, whose one desire was to bear witness to the truth, to give their lives for Him who had given His for them, to be faithful even unto death. And these brave men consoled His sacred Heart.

There was here in London a house of religious men, of whom it was commonly said that if it were possible that angels could live on earth in human flesh, they were to be found among the monks of the London Charterhouse. Of these men it might be said, as of my holy father St. Benedict, that they despised the world as a withered flower, only fit to be thrown away. Some had left great positions in the world, even the very king's court, to consecrate themselves to a life of prayer and austerity. These men were ready; they were faithful, and in them God found His consolation.

When the commissioners came to the London Charterhouse and summoned the monks to take the oath, the holy prior expressed his astonishment that a marriage sanctioned by the Holy See and consecrated by long years of undisputed intercourse should now be called in question. He and a companion were at once sent to the Tower. Here they were persuaded by theologians of repute that they might lawfully take the oath, with the condition attached, "as far as the law of Christ permits."[6] They were accordingly released, but the night before he left the prison Blessed John Houghton had a vision in which it was revealed to him that this was but a short respite, and that he would soon return to the Tower.[7] And indeed at the beginning of the next year (1535) a new Act came into force — that of Supremacy — and men were called upon to take an oath explicitly renouncing in the most

---

[6] It is unclear whether the Carthusians made the conditional oath "as far as the law of Christ permits" or were convinced by the arguments of theologians and bishops who came to them in prison.

[7] John Houghton was canonized a saint on 25 October 1970 as one of the 40 English and Welsh martyrs by Pope Paul VI.

offensive terms the jurisdiction of the Holy See, and acknowledging the king as Supreme Head of the Church.

As soon as this news reached him, the prior assembled his monks in the chapterhouse and told them the fatal tidings. It was evident that now there could be no compromise. Their hour had come. They were asked to renounce the Catholic faith, and it was clear that the penalty of refusal would be death — death in its most terrible form.

It was not death that he feared for them, however, but apostasy. He trembled lest some of his younger brethren should fail in the hour of trial, should return to the world, and thus imperil their salvation. "What shall I say then, brethren," he cried, "or what shall I do before the eternal judgment seat, if I cannot give a good account of those whom God has given me?"

The monks burst into tears, and cried out with one voice and one heart: "Let us all die in our innocency, and heaven and earth shall witness how unjustly we are cut off from the earth."

The holy prior was deeply moved; he declared that he was ready to lay down his life for the least of them, but he feared that this grace would not be granted him. He then exhorted them to prepare their hearts by a general confession, and permitted each to choose his own confessor. "And having done this," quoth he, "on the following day we will all be reconciled to each other, because without charity neither death nor life profiteth anything." And so, having reconciled themselves to God, they met in the chapterhouse, where the prior gave them a most pathetic sermon on charity and on patient and constant cleaving to God in adversity, concluding thus: "It is better to suffer here a short punishment for our faults than to be reserved for the eternal torments of hell."

Then he said: "Dearest brethren, I pray you all to do what you now see me do," and rising from his place, he went to the father vicar, who was sitting next to him, and kneeling down before him, humbly begged pardon for any offence which he might have committed against him in thought, word, or deed. Thus he did to all the religious in turn, shedding the while abundant tears. And they in like manner followed him, each asking pardon from all his brethren. And on the third day of this solemn triduum occurred a scene which is surpassed in pathetic and consoling beauty by no episode in all the Acts of the Saints. It is portrayed in the beautiful picture which hangs in the Oratory of the Martyrs. They met together, those white-robed monks, in their church — that little church of the London Charterhouse which still remains to us, an unspeakably precious relic of those heroic men. There, as they knelt in their stalls, the prior offered a solemn Mass of the Holy Ghost. As he raised aloft in sacrifice the immaculate Lamb of God, he united with that sacred Victim the offering of his own and of his brethren's blood.

"And during the time of the Mass," writes one who was present, "the almighty and merciful God deigned to work wondrous and ineffable things.[8] For when the most Sacred Host was lifted up, there came as it were a soft whisper of air, faint indeed to the outward senses, but of mighty power within the soul. Some perceived it with their bodily hearing; all felt it as it thrilled into their hearts. And there came a sound of melody most sweet, whereat the venerable prior was so moved that he melted into a flood of tears, and could not for a long space continue the offering of the Mass. The community meanwhile remained stupefied, hearing the melody and feeling its marvelous effects upon their spirits, but not knowing whence it came or whither it went. Yet their hearts rejoiced as they perceived that God was with them indeed." Thus, my brethren, did the all holy and merciful God deign to strengthen His servants for their last conflict, which was indeed nigh at hand.

The prior, hoping against hope, resolved to make one last appeal to Cromwell, to see if by chance he and his brethren might be exempted from the oath and allowed to serve God in peace. He therefore went with two brother priors, who had come to London to consult him, to visit the terrible vicegerent. But they were treated with scorn, and immediately committed to the Tower. When they pleaded the laws of the Catholic Church as their reason for refusing

---

[8] The "one who was present" was Dom Maurice Chauncy, a monk in the London Charterhouse. Chauncy was the last monk of the London Charterhouse (after 18 others had been martyred) to take the oath. He regretted passing the crown of martyrdom the rest of his life, but did leave us several accounts of the last days of St. John Houghton and his companions.

the oath, Cromwell roughly answered: "What do I care for the Church?"

It was the first time that such words had been heard in Catholic England, and they were a fitting prelude to all that was to follow. Henceforth the whim of a tyrannical monarch was to be the supreme law for Church and State.

At their trial the holy priors again refused the oath, but the jury refused to stain their hands in innocent blood by bringing in a verdict of "Guilty." It was not till Cromwell had himself visited them and threatened them with horrible penalties that he secured his end.

And so on May 4, 1535, a prisoner stood at his window in the Tower of London when he beheld a strange sight — a sight such as had never yet been seen in England. There were these heroic monks, still clad in their religious habits, stretched on hurdles to be dragged to Tyburn. "See," he cried to his daughter, who stood beside him; "see how these blessed fathers be now as cheerfully going to their deaths as bridegrooms to their marriage."

And the Blessed Thomas More (for it was he) envied the martyrs with a holy envy, for they were now about to grasp their crown.

And so they came to Tyburn, to this very spot where now we stand, where the great triangular gibbet stood out black against the sky, to Tyburn the Golgotha of England, like the first Golgotha a place of ignominy and shame, but henceforth to be glorious beyond all the shrines of England, glorious like that "place of a skull" on which the King of Martyrs died. Who shall describe the scene when the protomartyrs of Tyburn came here to win their crown? We can picture it from the accounts of eyewitnesses. The vast crowd; a sea of heads stretching on all sides as far as eye could see; in the midst close to the gibbet a group of horsemen, nobles from the court, with their faces masked by black visors (it was whispered that the king himself had come to feast his eyes on the agonies of his victims[9]), the fearful preparations for the coming

---

[9] It was rumored, but the rumor has been found to be untrue. In all likelihood, the masked horsemen were from Henry VIII's court but Henry himself was not among them.

butchery —the cauldron, the knives, the quartering block — we can see it all before us as the martyrs are dragged up to the foot of their Calvary, their white robes splashed with the mire of the rough and filthy roads, their faces worn with pain but radiant with the light of victory.

"I am ready," cried the blessed prior, "to suffer every kind of torture rather than deny a doctrine of the Church. Pray for me, and have mercy on my brethren of whom I have been the unworthy prior." And then, commending himself to God in the words of his dying Lord, he submitted himself sweetly to the indescribable butchery that followed. The rope by which he hung was quickly cut, and the body still breathing fell heavily on the ground. The sacred habit was brutally torn off and the martyr's body ripped open by the cruel knife. He was heard to cry, "Oh, most holy Jesus, have mercy on me in this hour." And when at last the executioner placed his hand upon the heart, ready to tear it from his breast, "Good Jesu," he murmured, "what will ye do with my heart?"

Good Jesu, what wilt Thou do with his heart, with this brave heart which has been true to Thee till death? What wilt Thou do with it? Wilt Thou not enshrine it among Thy choicest treasures very near Thine own? Shall it not be hidden in the wound of that most Sacred Heart, a heart that has ever beaten for Thee alone, a heart that is sacrificed thus for Thy love? Will it not bring Thee consolation amid the suffering inflicted on Thy Heart by the miserable apostasy of so many who professed to be Thy friends? Here at least is one who in reply to Thine invitation has literally given Thee his heart, one who has been faithful even unto death, one who has died for love of Thee who died for love of him!

It was thus that the protomartyr of Tyburn witnessed a good confession, and his sons were not slow to follow in his steps. There is the Blessed Sebastian, young and fair and noble, once the darling of the royal court and now the model of monastic virtues. When his good sister warned him of the dangers of the court, he scarcely believed her, and yet even then he was meditating on his flight to the Charterhouse. And she who doubted his strength and resolution for a life so austere, lived to see him constant and joyous in the midst of unheard of tortures, chained upright in his dungeon, unable to move hand or foot for a whole fortnight before the sharp torments of Tyburn united him to his Father once more. There are the glorious brethren, priests and lay-brothers alike, who were thrown into the horrible and fetid dungeons of Newgate. There they were deliberately left to perish of hunger, chained to the walls and pillars of their dungeon, and deprived of all human succor. Even Henry shrank from the odium he would have incurred had he dared to have them openly butchered at Tyburn. He therefore commanded that they should be left in chains to rot like dogs.

But there was one, (may her name be held in everlasting remembrance); a woman who, in the household of Sir Thomas More, had learnt the spirit of the early martyrs, and who came, at the risk of her life, to minister to God's servants in their need. She disguised herself as a milkmaid, and having bribed the jailer to allow her access to the martyrs, fed that blessed company from a pail which she carried on her head, putting the food into their mouths as they were unable to move hand or foot. She then would clean out the fetid dungeon, and in this noble work of charity she persevered for some time, till the king made inquiries why they were not yet dead, and commanded a closer watch to be kept over them. Thus she was no longer allowed admission, but even then she contrived to go to the tiles right over the prison, and making a hole in the roof to let down by a string a basket of food, which she approached as well as she could to their mouths. But in the end, the jailer was afraid to allow her to come, and so soon after, the martyrs languished and pined away, one after the other, and went to receive their crown in heaven. Nor were they ungrateful to the heroic woman who had shown them charity in their hour of need. As Margaret Clement lay dying at Mechlin, an exile for the faith, she called her husband and told him that the time of her departure was come and she might stay no longer, for that there were standing about her bed the blessed martyrs of the London Charterhouse whom she had relieved in prison in England, and they were calling on her to come away with them. And this she told also to her confessor and to others who were with her, her countenance smiling and full of heavenly joy; and thus she was escorted by that blessed company to the joys of the heavenly banquet.

Did not these men, my brethren, console the Heart of God?

And shall we, who are their children, not strive to follow in their steps? We cannot all be monks or nuns in the cloister, nor is that necessary; wherever God has placed us there we can console Him by our fidelity.

It is true that things are very easy for us now. We have no martyrdom to fear, no tortures to undergo for the love of Christ. The more shame then to us if we do not give Him our hearts! We have all some work to do for Him, all something to bear for His love. It may be that our faith prevents our getting on in this world as otherwise we might; it may well be that from time to time at least we may have to bear scorn and ridicule, coldness and dislike for that same holy faith; to converts especially is it often granted, even in these days of toleration and indifference, to suffer somewhat — loss of friends, loss of goods and money, perhaps — for the love of Christ.

Oh, how happy are those who are thus permitted to taste something of the martyrs' chalice; how earnestly we ought to thank God if we are thus permitted to show Him that our love is real, that it will stand the test of suffering, and ring true in the midst of persecution.

Yes, let us be true to Him in spite of the sneers of an indifferent world; let us cling to His sacred feet, and let no temptation drive us from them; let us by our fidelity, even unto death, console that Sacred Heart which is too often wounded in the house of its friends. Then may we hope to meet the blessed martyrs in paradise, and to be numbered among those happy ones in whom our God shall ever find His consolation.

II

The Martyrs Champions of the Holy See

Monday, May 2, 1904

"Tu es Petrus, et super hanc petram aedificabo ecclesiam meam et portae inferi non praevalebunt adversus eam. — Thou art Peter, and upon this rock I will build my Church, and the gates of hell shall not prevail against it." — Matt. 16: 18.

IT was indeed a memorable occasion: that day at Caesarea Phillippi, when Andrew brought his brother Simon to Jesus, and He, looking with loving and prophetic eyes on the young man kneeling at His feet, addressed him by a new name, symbolic of the office and dignity he was to bear in His Church. "Thou art Simon, son of John," He said: "Thou shalt be called Peter the Rock, and upon thee as upon a rock will I build My Church, and the gates, that is, the powers of hell, shall never prevail against it, for it is built upon the Rock, and therefore shall it stand unharmed until the end of time. And unto thee, O Peter, will I give the keys, that is, the supreme authority on earth over my Church which is the Kingdom of Heaven here below, and thou shalt have power to open and to shut, to bind and to loose: all thy judgments shall be ratified and confirmed in heaven, for thou art to be my vicegerent on earth."

This wondrous promise was made by the Son of God, by Him who is Truth itself, who can neither deceive nor be deceived. And in this blessed Paschal-time the promise thus made at Caesarea was fulfilled, when Peter, kneeling in loving self-abasement at his Master's feet, received by the shores of the Galilean lake the charge of the whole flock of Christ. To his care were then entrusted the sheep and the lambs, that dear and precious flock which Jesus had bought with His own most precious Blood, but which He was now about to leave. And ever since that day there has always been one sitting in Peter's chair, to whose care, as Vicar of his Master, the sheep of Christ were committed.

The Church of God has been entrusted by the Divine Will to one supreme shepherd for the preservation, of unity and the defense of the flock from the ravages of schism and heresy. His it is to rule and govern in the name of Christ, his to unfold the oracles of God, his to condemn errors as they arise, to feed the flock with life-giving pastures and to guide them in the way of salvation. He is the divinely appointed guardian of the oracles of God, the supreme judge in matters of faith and morals, the head of the Church on earth, whose power no man may usurp, whose rights no man may question. And this successor of St. Peter, this vicar of the Savior of the world, we call our holy Lord and Father the Pope.

Nowhere in Christendom was there more passionate and devoted loyalty to the successor of St. Peter than here in England. Our Saxon fathers never forgot how strong and tender a tie bound them to Rome and Peter's chair. They gloried in the fact that they alone of the nations of Christendom could boast of having a Pope as their apostle. They never wearied in proclaiming their undying gratitude to that holy Pontiff, Gregory the Great, who had sent to their fathers the faith of Christ and the gift of Baptism. The roads to Rome were worn by the feet of countless English pilgrims. Our greatest saints, such as Bede, Wilfrid, Boniface, Benet Biscop and Aldhelm, could not say or do enough to express their reverence and submission to the See of Peter, from which, as they loved to recall, their Christianity had sprung.

We still remember with love, as our fathers did, that most blessed Pope who from the day that he first saw those English slave boys exposed for sale in the Roman Forum, cherished in his heart so deep and constant a love for our country, so eager a desire to win it to the faith of Jesus Christ. True it is that Gregory never trod these shores, but none the less we recognize that the instinct of our Saxon fathers who claimed him as their apostle was a true one. They knew how he had longed to rescue them from the wrath of God and to teach them to sing the celestial Alleluia; they loved to recount how he had indeed set out for England but had been recalled ere he had gone four days' journey, in order that he might rule over the flock of Christ. And then when raised aloft upon Peter's Chair he had still borne our country in his heart, still labored for its conversion, hoping, as he himself wrote to Augustine, that he might share in the reward of his labors, since he had so earnestly desired to share in the toil. And thus the love and gratitude of our fathers rings out in the words of their great doctor and historian. "We may and we ought to call the blessed Gregory our apostle," writes St. Bede, "for though to others he was not an apostle, nevertheless he is so to us, for we are the seal of his apostleship in the Lord." And so the English Church assembled in solemn synod in the seventh century decreed that the feast of this blessed Pope, her apostle, should ever be kept as a day of obligation, and that the names of Gregory and Augustine should ever be solemnly invoked in the Litanies of the Saints. And we remember with emotion the name of that English prince who, renouncing his kingdom together with his pagan faith, journeyed in pilgrimage to the threshold of the apostles, in order that he might there receive at the hands of the successor of St. Peter the sacrament of regeneration, and dying there, still clad in his chrisom robe, was laid to rest at the feet of the great Gregory, the apostle of his race. There they found him in the seventeenth century, at the time of the rebuilding of the Vatican Basilica — truly a touching emblem of England's ancient faith and ancient love.

If in Norman days that love grew somewhat colder, still, thank God, there were always saints among us to bear witness to the truth. There was the meek and constant Anselm; there was Thomas, the fearless, the invincible; and many another who stood up before kings and princes, and even before the craven pastors of the flock, willing and desirous to lay down their lives for the prerogatives of Peter, witnessing to the faith which Augustine brought from Rome, in deeds not less clear than words.

And so, in the dark days of which I spoke yesterday, God raised up among us faithful and stalwart champions of the Holy See.

State-rule in faith, they knew, means heresy,
That truth they wrote in blood and closed debate
By acts, not words.

The truth to which they witnessed may be summed up in the words of the Venerable Bede, speaking as he does for the old Church of old England, of which he was the brightest light.

"Blessed Peter received in a special manner the keys of the kingdom of Heaven and the chiefship of judicial power, that all believers throughout the world might understand that whosoever separate themselves in any way whatever from the unity of the faith or from his communion, can neither be absolved from the bonds of their sins nor enter within the gate of the kingdom of heaven." And many centuries later the Church of England in Synod assembled thus solemnly defined her faith. "Christ ordained St. Peter the apostle to be His vicar here on earth, whose See is the Church of Rome, ordaining and granting that the same power He gave to Peter should succeed to all Peter's successors, the which we now call popes of Rome, by whose power be ordained prelates to whom Christian men ought to obey after the laws of the Church of Rome."

These martyrs of ours, whom we are met here to celebrate, form a glorious army of witnesses to this ancient faith, such as no other Church in Christendom can boast. When more than fifty years ago the question of the restoration of our ancient hierarchy was being discussed at Rome, it was objected in some quarters that to establish bishops with ordinary or diocesan jurisdiction in place of vicars apostolic, with authority delegated from Rome, would perhaps tend to weaken the ties that bound our English Church to the Holy See. To this the absolutely triumphant answer was at once ready. The English Church, it was replied — and she alone could make such a boast — had given, during a period of persecution lasting one hundred and fifty years, and unexampled for ferocity, more than three hundred martyrs who had poured out their blood like water for the rights of the apostolic See. This was conclusive. Thus the martyrs secured for us the priceless boon of the hierarchy just as they had already preserved for us the still more sacred treasure of the faith.

But let us take as examples one or two of this white-robed army. If the question had been asked in the reign of Henry VIII as to who was the most famous, the most brilliant, the most successful, and the most devout of all the laymen of England, there is not the least doubt as to what the answer would have been. The inquirer would have been told on all sides that there was no one to compare with Sir Thomas More, Lord High Chancellor of England. Indeed, I think that this glorious man occupies a unique place among our martyrs. Most of them were priests or religious, men who had already given up the world and its pleasures, and whom therefore we should have expected to be ready when the call came to give up even life itself for the love of Christ; but More, on the contrary, was a man with wife and family, a happy home circle which he most tenderly loved, and to part with which was more bitter than death itself. Yet he never swerved nor flinched — no, not for a moment; ever steadfast, ever faithful, ever bright and joyous, indeed, as our poet has sung:

A dauntless soul erect that smiled on death.

It is not, however, necessary for me to praise this incomparable man. He has been the object of the passionate admiration of men who shared not his faith and loved not the cause for which he died. A well known Protestant statesman thus spoke of him not long ago: "The greatest of great Englishmen, the most justly famed of English lives.... Of all men nearly perfect, nay, of all saints, let me say, for if ever one of God's saints walked the earth it was Sir Thomas More. . . . No beatification can add to, no human praise or blame could alter, the noble historical character of the man."

The Blessed Thomas More is then one of the most glorious witnesses to the Holy Roman Faith. When the call of duty came, and he had to choose between the faith which he had learned at his mother's knee on the one hand, and on the other the glamour of a great position, and all that the world holds dear and precious, he did not hesitate for an instant, but went with a cheerful smile to his death, mounting the scaffold with a blithe face and a merry jest, rejoicing that he was counted worthy to suffer for the name of

Christ. It was More who said that "a man can live for the next world and yet be merry"; which has well been called "one of the most beautiful sayings of all time." He had foreseen his fall; even when basking in the brightest sunshine of the royal favor, his eyes were not blinded nor his heart seduced. When he succeeded Cardinal Wolsey as Lord Chancellor, he publicly compared his position to that of Damocles, who sat at the king's table with a sword hanging by a hair above his head. He "put not his trust in princes nor in any child of man," and was not a whit moved when he saw the very stars of heaven fall, and the pillars of the firmament tottering around him. The clergy and people of England might renounce their faith; he at least would be true. When the king summoned him and his fellow martyr, Bishop Fisher, "to swear to the statute made against the pope, six weeks being given them to consider the matter, they replied that they were ready to suffer what martyrdom pleased the king, and that they would not change their opinion in six weeks, or even in six hundred years, if they lived so long."

He had long been preparing his family for the blow. He had told them "of the holy martyrs of the ancient Church, of their grievous pains, of their marvelous patience, and of their passions and deaths, that they suffered rather than they would offend almighty God, and what a happy and blessed thing it was for the love of God to suffer loss of goods and imprisonment, loss of lands and life also. That upon his faith, if he might perceive his wife and children would encourage him to die in so good a cause, it should comfort him, that for very joy thereof it would make him run merrily to death."

Unhappily, even this consolation was denied him. As he lay in his gloomy dungeon in the Tower of London, his wife came and scolded him for ruining his family by his foolish obstinacy, and allowing himself to be shut up in a loathsome prison when he might be enjoying the king's favor and living at ease in his beautiful home at Chelsea. He heard her with a cheerful countenance, and asked her: "Is not this house as nigh heaven as my own?" Then he asked, supposing he were to do as she wished and sacrifice his conscience and return to live at Chelsea, how long a life could she promise him? And when she answered, "Ah, well, you might live twenty years yet," he smilingly said, "O Ah, it is you who are foolish; if you could have promised me twenty thousand years — and yet what are even twenty thousand years compared with eternity?"

When he was a young man, with all his life before him, he had written a treatise on the Four Last Things, and ever throughout life he had kept the end of man steadily before him. "Remember thy last end, and thou shalt never sin," sounded continually in his ears; and, as he told his beloved daughter Margaret Roper, when she came to visit him in his cell, if it had not been for the dear ties of home and family, he would long ago have shut himself up in an even straighter cell; meaning, as it seems, that he would have become a Carthusian monk. While in his prison he wrote his beautiful "Dialogue of Comfort in Tribulation," which has comforted so many sufferers in later days, and a treatise on the Passion of Christ. It is touching to note that he had reached the words, "Then laid they their hands on Jesus to take Him away," when the book abruptly ceases, for his time had come. When they took away from him his books and writing materials he closed the shutters of his dungeon, and remained in the dark in order that he might the better meditate without distraction on the love and Passion of his Lord.

We saw how he had watched and had envied the blessed Carthusian priors going to martyrdom "like bridegrooms to the marriage," and how he lamented to his beloved daughter that "God thought him not worthy to come so soon to that eternal felicity, but left him still in this world further to be plagued and turmoiled with misery"; but it was not to be for long. The servile Parliament had passed the Act of Supremacy while More lay in prison, and now men came and read it to him. It decreed that whosoever should attempt maliciously to deprive the king of his title of Supreme Head of the Church of England, either by word, writing or imagination (for in those days of tyranny even a man's thoughts were no longer free!) should be held guilty of High Treason and punished by the terrible death reserved to traitors. When it was sought to entangle our blessed martyr in the meshes of this iniquitous law, he behaved with dignity and Christian prudence. He refused to give a direct answer, saying: "I will not meddle with any such matters, for I am fully determined to serve God and to think upon His Passion and my passage out of this world"; and he wrote to Bishop Fisher, his fellow prisoner: "The Act of Parliament is like a sword with two edges: for if a man answer one way it will confound his soul, and if he answer the other way it will confound his body." Yet these answers were the only proofs of treason which they could bring against our martyr at his trial. Nay, there was one thing more, and that was the evidence of a false witness; that in his sufferings he might be the more conformed to the likeness of his divine Master.

Rich, the Solicitor General, deposed against him that he had had a conversation with him in the Tower, in which he said, "Supposing Parliament should enact that I, Richard Rich, should be king, would you accept me as such?" To this More replied, "Yes," whereupon Rich continued, "and supposing they made me pope, what then?" More replied by another question, "Supposing it were enacted by Parliament that God was not God, would you agree to that?" "Certainly not," said Rich, whereupon the martyr remained silent. Rich, however, had the effrontery to swear that he replied, "Neither can the Parliament declare that the pope is not head of the Church."

Blessed Thomas was determined that he would in no sense court death, or go to a judicial suicide. He knew that such was not the spirit in which a martyr of Christ should go to meet his end. He therefore made a magnificent defense at his trial, a defense worthy of his great reputation as a barrister. He declared that he was more sorry for Rich's perjury than for his own peril. Nevertheless, when once condemned to death, he thought it his duty to bear solemn witness to the faith for which he died. He then spoke out boldly the dearest convictions of his soul. Never surely did those old rafters at Westminster Hall echo to so noble a confession! Standing there as a condemned criminal, there, where he had so often presided as supreme judge, in all the pomp of his high office, he proclaimed the truth (and the voice of England's ancient Church spoke through his lips), that the supremacy over the kingdom of God on earth could belong to no layman, but that it "rightfully belonged to the See of Rome as granted personally by our Lord when on earth to St. Peter and his successors," that for England to refuse obedience to Rome was the same as for a child to refuse obedience to its natural parent. For as St. Paul said to the Corinthians, "Ye are my children, for I have begotten you in Christ," so might St. Gregory say to the English, "Ye are my children, for I have, under Christ, given to you everlasting salvation." "You taunt me," he went on, "that I stand here alone, that all the great and learned men of England are against me. I tell you that for one bishop of your opinion I have a hundred saints of mine, and for one parliament of yours, and God knows of what kind, I have all the General Councils of a thousand years, and for one kingdom I have France and all the kingdoms of Christendom; yea, and on my side I have all the saints in heaven!" Yet even now, as ever, he was playful and sweet, and he ended by expressing his hope "that as St. Paul and St. Stephen, whom he persecuted, were now friends in paradise, so he and his judges, though differing in this world, might be united in perfect charity in the next."

And so he left the Hall with the axe's edge turned towards him, in sign that he was a condemned traitor, but with joy on his countenance and God's peace in his heart. Only once did his composure fail him, and that was when at the Tower steps he found his beloved daughter Margaret waiting to bid him farewell. We know, from her husband's pathetic narrative, how that faithful daughter burst through the guards who surrounded her father and fell upon his neck, crying, "Oh, my father, oh, my father!" He embraced her and blessed her with a heart too full for words, and then, as he was being led away, she ran to him once more and enfolded him in a long embrace, sobbing out her heart upon his breast. We know what comfort she gave him in that supreme hour, for when he reached the prison he wrote to her some loving words of comfort, traced with a coal from the fire — for the tyrant had deprived him of pen and ink. In this he says: "If I were to declare in writing how much pleasure your daughterly, loving behavior gave me, a peck of coals would not suffice to make the pens!"

To this dear daughter, surely the noblest Englishwoman who ever lived and worthy of such a father, he sent just before his martyrdom his instruments of penance, his discipline and hairshirt, used assiduously to the last but now no longer needed, with a touching letter of farewell, in which he lovingly blessed her and all his children, adding, "I cumber you, good Margaret, much, but I would be sorry that it should be any longer than tomorrow, for it is St. Thomas's eve, and the octave of St. Peter, and therefore tomorrow long I to go to God." It was indeed a fitting day for the sacrifice, the eve of the translation of his own glorious patron St. Thomas; on what better day could he be translated from earth to Heaven, he who belonged by closest ties of confraternity to the Cathedral Monastery of the Martyr at Canterbury; he who was to die for that selfsame cause for which St. Thomas shed his blood? On what better day again than on the octave of the feast of the great Prince of the Apostles, for whose prerogative he was giving his life? And so it was indeed, for on this day he was led out to die. He had entered the prison house fifteen months before in the strength and prime of manhood; he left it now a broken, grey haired man, made old before his time by the rigors of his imprisonment.

The horrors of Tyburn had been spared him, and by a special exercise of the royal "mercy" he was to die by the axe on Tower Hill. As he went forth, holding to his heart a small red cross, a good woman offered him a cup of wine, but he refused it, saying: "My Lord drank only vinegar and gall." A poor man, who had known him of old, came and knelt at his feet, begging his prayers. He was sorely tried with terrible temptations to despair, constantly impelled to lay violent hands upon himself. The martyr said to him, "Go and pray for me, and I will pray for thee." And from that hour the man was wholly delivered from his trial. Even at the foot of the scaffold he retained his old playful humor, and observing that the ladder shook beneath him, he said to the lieutenant of the Tower, "I pray thee see me safe up, and I will shift for myself coming down." And after praying by the block, he kissed the executioner in token of forgiveness, saying, "Pluck up thy spirits, man, and be not afraid to do thy office. My neck is very short, take heed therefore that thou strike not awry for thy honor's sake." Thus, with a smile on his lips and forgiveness in his heart, he patiently submitted to the death stroke, and so his blessed spirit passed to God.

More had said once to his children, "You see virtue rewarded and vice punished, so that you are carried up to heaven even by the chins. But if you live in the time when you shall see virtue punished and vice rewarded, if you will then stand fast and firmly stick to God, if you be but half good, God will allow you for whole good." Was he not indeed one of those true friends of God who, as we saw yesterday, console the Sacred Heart? Never did there beat a heart so true and loyal, never a friend so staunch in storm as in the sunshine.

But let us turn for a moment to the Blessed John Fisher, More's faithful friend in life and companion in martyrdom.[10] He was revered by all as the most saintly and apostolic bishop in England, if not in Christendom. He had passed the allotted span of man's life, and was so weak and sickly that it was deemed a wonderful thing that he should have survived his long imprisonment. As he wrote to Cromwell, he suffered cruelly during the long months he spent in the Bell Tower from cold and want of suitable food. His clothes were in rags, and his body so frail and wasted that he seemed more dead than alive. He was once taken so ill that his death was expected daily, and the king then sent to him his own physician, not indeed from any sense of pity, but in order, if possible, to preserve him for the scaffold. Anne Boleyn had vowed a terrible vengeance against the bishop: she thirsted for his blood as did Herodias of old for that of another John.

When the Pope heard that this venerable prelate lay in prison, daily expecting death for the cause of the Apostolic See, he was greatly moved, and, calling a solemn consistory, he created him a cardinal priest of the Holy Roman Church, thinking that even Henry's impiety would shrink from laying violent hands on a prince of the Church. But this news only inflamed the monarch's rage the more, and he exclaimed with an oath, "The Pope may send him a cardinal's hat if he will, but he will have to wear it on his shoulders, for I will take care that he has not a head to put it on." He sent Cromwell to the prison to ask the holy bishop what he would do if the Pope were to send him the hat, and the martyr's reply, "I would receive it on my knees," did not serve to abate the royal fury.

---

[10] John Fisher was canonized a saint on 19 May 1935.

Fisher died with calm dignity and holy joy, on a most fitting festival, that of St. Alban our protomartyr. He was so weak that he had to be carried in a chair to the scaffold. During this sad procession he took the little Greek testament which he always carried with him, and asked our Lord to give him some comfort at the supreme hour. He opened it at the text, "This is life eternal to know Thee the one true God, and Jesus Christ whom Thou hast sent." And then he shut the book, saying, "Here is comfort enough." As he painfully mounted the scaffold the June sun shone full in his face, and the old man raised up his arms to heaven, crying, "*Accedite ad eum et illuminamini, et fades vestrce non confundentur* — Draw near unto Him and be enlightened, and your faces shall not be confounded." (Ps. 33:6)

Alas, the headless body of the holy cardinal was allowed to lie naked on the scaffold the whole day, till in the evening two soldiers took it up on their halberds and tumbled it into a grave without prayer or sign of reverence. It is even asserted that Anne Boleyn had the severed head brought to her that she might exult over it. "But the souls of the righteous are in the hand of God, and there shall no torment touch them."

Such, my brethren, were the noble leaders of the martyrs of England; but there followed in their footsteps a whole army of white-robed witnesses. There were priests and laymen, young men and maidens, old men and matrons — yes, and children too, who refused to bow down before the golden idol of the royal supremacy, and joyously suffered all that human malice could inflict rather than deny the faith.

There is, for instance, the Venerable George Haydock, imprisoned for the faith, but so far from being daunted by his sufferings that he writes up on the very walls of his dungeon the triumphant inscription, "Gregory XIII, supreme head on earth of the whole Catholic Church," and stoutly refuses, when commanded, to erase what he has written. There is young Thomas Sherwood protesting on the rack that "The Pope and he alone is God's general vicar on earth," and keeping to his brave confession even when thrust down into a frightful underground dungeon "among the rats." There is Blessed John Felton, hacked in pieces before the gates of the Protestant Bishop of London because he had dared to hang

40

upon those very gates the sentence of St. Pius V, excommunicating Elizabeth as an apostate and a heretic. There is young Robert Ashton, butchered for seeking a marriage dispensation from the Holy See, and the priest Polydore Plasden, who here at Tyburn with the rope already round his neck is once more urged to renounce the faith. "Oh Christ," he cries, looking up to heaven, "Oh Christ, I will not deny Thee for a thousand lives." There again is the Blessed John Forest, condemned to the flames as a heretic by the apostate Cranmer because, forsooth, he maintained in word and writing the primacy of the Apostolic See. There too is a little group of knights of St. John who knew how to withstand the tyranny of the royal heretic as bravely as did their brethren the inrush of the Mussulman invader. There are the Blessed Benedictine abbots, true to Christ and Rome as were their fathers before them, and shedding an imperishable luster upon the desolate ruins of their venerable abbeys. There are the sons of SS. Francis of Assisi and Ignatius of Loyola, hand in hand with the ardent missioners from Allen's glorious foundations, treading joyously in the steps of the King of Martyrs, and for the joy that was set before them despising the shame of their Calvary. All these form part of that great host of victorious warriors who have come through great tribulation to the peace of paradise. And now, me-thinks, I see them standing around the throne of Peter in heaven, and as they wave aloft their palms, they blend their voices in the triumphant antiphon, "*Tu es pastor ovium, princes apostolorum, tibi traditae sunt claves regni caelorum* — Thou art the shepherd of the sheep, the prince of the apostles: to thee are delivered the keys of the kingdom of heaven, alleluia."

My brethren, the Martyrs of Tyburn teach us the duty of devotion to the Apostolic See. This devotion has ever been a special mark of God's saints, and as de Maistre has observed, the more conspicuous was their sanctity, the more remarkable were they for love of Rome and of all that comes from Rome.

We should cherish a love for the Apostolic See as a very special grace from God; and if we find we have it not we should earnestly pray for it. In these days especially, when the canker of criticism and independence seems to be spreading its ravages so seriously even among Catholics, we must seek to possess this spirit of childlike submission and love for Rome. All around us are good people who call themselves by the glorious title of Catholic, which is nevertheless the inalienable heritage of those who abide in the communion and fellowship of the Apostolic See, and of them alone.

These men say that they believe all that we believe, with the solitary exception of the Primacy of Peter. But this exception is fatal to their claim to the Catholic name. They may indeed accept our doctrines, but they do so merely on their own authority, as matters of private judgment. We Catholics, on the contrary, believe them with divine faith, on the authority of the Church of God, which is the organ and mouthpiece of the Holy Ghost; and we know that to reject even one of them is to reject all and to make shipwreck of the Faith. We know that to Peter and to his successors has the supreme authority been committed ; that to accept all that they teach, because it commends itself to our reason, and at the same time to reject the authority of the teacher, is to proclaim oneself a Protestant, devoid of either faith or logic. We must never let ourselves be deceived by special pleading; those who are not firmly grounded on the Rock of Peter cannot belong to the Church of Christ, however near it they may seem to be. The martyrs teach us that there can be no compromise on this point: to attempt it indeed would be no real charity; it would be but to deceive those dear souls for whose conversion we long. We must be full of charity for them, but at the same time absolutely firm as to the essentials. And for ourselves, let us thank God with all our hearts that He has given us a supreme and infallible teacher to guide us on the road to heaven and to point out to us with unfaltering voice the perils that beset us on the way. Let us cling to the Rock of Peter and glory in the name of Papist, which is so often applied to us by those who love us not, but which is in fact a title of honor for the disciple of Jesus. Yes, we are Papists, and we love our Pope; we glory in his prerogative and find our joy and consolation in his teaching. We know that as long as we are united to him we are safe, that we belong to the fold of Christ against which the gates of hell shall never prevail; and, amid all the trials and sorrows of life, who shall rob us of this supreme consolation? The good shepherd knoweth his sheep by name, and they hear his voice, and to us as to St. Alphonsus "the voice of the Pope is the voice of God."

Let me conclude with the dying words of one of our glorious martyrs: "The supremacy hath and doth belong to the Pope by right derived from Peter, and the Pope hath received it as by divine providence. Therefore, we must not give those things belonging to God to any other than Him alone. And because I will not do otherwise, I may say with the three children in the fiery furnace and the first of the widow's seven sons in the Maccabees: 'Parati sumus mori magis quam patrias Dei leges praevaricari.'"

Yes, by God's grace, we too are "prepared to die rather than depart from the laws of God which our fathers have handed down to us."

III

The Martyrs Witnesses to the Holy Mass

Tuesday, May 3, 1904

"Thou shalt offer thy oblations, the Flesh and the Blood upon the altar of the Lord thy God, and the Flesh thou thyself shalt eat . . . and thou wilt eat the Flesh thy soul desireth." - Deut. 12:27 and 12:20
"They shall violate My secret place and robbers shall enter in and shall defile it... They have defiled My sanctuaries. And I was profaned in the midst of them."- Ezec 7:22 and 22:26.

These words of the prophet, my brethren, are very appropriate to the subject of which I have to speak to you today — the witness of our blessed martyrs to the Holy Sacrifice of the Mass. After the doctrine of the primacy of the Apostolic See, of which I spoke yesterday, there is no dogma of the faith to which the martyrs of England bore more emphatic witness, none for which they poured out their blood so abundantly, as that of the adorable sacrifice of the altar.

Let us consider for a moment what the sacrifice of the Mass really is. It is to the Church of God what the sun in the heavens is to this earth of ours. What would be the effect on this globe could that mighty orb be suddenly extinguished? Would not the world be plunged into darkness, frozen with cold? The beautiful flowers would droop and die, the trees lose their leaves, the birds and beasts would perish, and we ourselves could not long survive them. So would the Church on earth be deprived of heavenly light and heat, if the most Divine Sacrifice be abolished from Her midst.

It is by this adorable sacrifice that the presence of Jesus is ever ensured to her, and it is in this most pure oblation that His all-prevailing merits are constantly pleaded with God on behalf of sinful man. We sometimes wonder how it is that God can be so patient; how it is that He does not strike the earth with the lightning of His wrath, and destroy once more a race whose iniquities are constantly crying out to heaven for vengeance? The answer to this mystery is to be found in the sacrifice of the Mass. If God remains silent when men deny Him to the face, if He bears so long with their rebellion, their ingratitude, their impurity; it is because there is never a moment of time when from some point of this globe the immaculate Lamb of God is not lifted up between heaven and earth in the hands of some humble priest; and the Father, looking upon the face of His beloved Son in whom He is ever well pleased, for His dear sake and for His blood outpoured and for His open wounds has pity on the race that dear Son died to save.

Thus it was in the old Greek story. A tyrant, who by his cruelty had long made his name odious, had at last to fly from the just indignation of his own people. But he had nowhere to turn for refuge, save to the land of a king whom he had in the past most cruelly wronged. It was to this man's house he fled, and entering in found none but the women and the king's infant son lying in a cradle by the fire. He went and sat down as a suppliant among the ashes on the hearth. And presently the king came in, and seeing his old enemy there humbled before him and wholly at his mercy, was filled with exultation, and raised his weapon to strike him to the earth. But the suppliant snatched up the innocent babe from the cradle and held him up in his arms between himself and the avenger. And the father, looking upon the face of his beloved child, was touched with compassion, and took his enemy in his arms, giving him the kiss of peace. Thus for the sake of the innocent child a father pardoned his foe, and thus is the great heart of God moved and His just anger averted by the offering of His Son and the perpetual pleading of the sacrifice of Calvary.

We saw on Sunday the protomartyrs of Tyburn cheered and strengthened for their conflict in the sacrifice of the Holy Mass. This adorable sacrifice was indeed most dear to all our martyrs. The great man of whom I spoke to you yesterday, Blessed Thomas

More, was conspicuous for his devotion to the Holy Mass. Even when Lord High Chancellor of England, he deemed it his highest privilege to don a surplice and serve Mass in his parish church.[11]

The Duke of Norfolk once surprised him when engaged in this sacred office. "God's body, my Lord Chancellor! What a parish clerk, a parish clerk! You dishonor the king and his office," he cried. "Nay," replied the martyr, smiling, "your Grace should not think that the king, your master and mine, will be offended with me for serving God his master." At another time, when hearing Mass, he was suddenly summoned to the king's presence, but he refused to leave the church until the Holy Sacrifice was completed. He knew that even the royal business was as nothing compared with the importance of the Mass.

He showed his love to the Holy Sacrifice by richly endowing the chapel which he built in his parish church at Chelsea with costly ornaments and plate. As he was wont to say: "Good men give these things and bad men take them away."

So it was that when he was summoned to Lambeth to meet the crisis of his fate he first went quietly to the church, and there having made his confession, devoutly assisted at Mass and received Holy Communion. It was in the strength of this Sacrifice that he went forth to combat for the faith; it was by the grace of this Sacrifice that he was enabled, after but a short struggle with nature, to regain his old joyousness and to whisper to the faithful companion who sat by him in the boat, "Son Roper, I thank our Lord, the field is won."

And if a layman so loved and valued the adorable Sacrament of the altar, what shall we say of those devoted priests who suffered here in England? To celebrate Holy Mass was to them the chief joy of life, the very end of their existence. We read of Blessed John Houghton that he was wont to shed copious tears as he offered the divine mysteries; and of Blessed Hugh, abbot of

---

[11] It is touching to know that these Masses served by a martyr were also offered by a martyr; for the Blessed John Larke, parish priest of Chelsea, followed in the footsteps of his own disciple, and consummated a glorious martyrdom at Tyburn.

Reading, we are told that in the dark days of trial it was his one consolation to offer daily the Holy Sacrifice for the peace of the Church and the good estate of the Roman Pontiff.

To do him justice, Henry VIII had no intention of making war upon the Mass. On the contrary he persecuted the heretics who dared to speak against the sacrifice, and in his last will he left provision for perpetual Masses for his soul. But by his obstinacy and self-will he had torn England from the centre of unity, and whether he willed it or no, the fatal consequences of such a step were soon to become apparent. He had removed the keystone of the arch, and the whole structure was bound quickly to crumble into ruin. When men create a schism, they are taking the first steps of a downward path which sooner or later leads inevitably to the depths of heresy. We have seen this truth exemplified in our own day in the history of the sect called the "Old Catholics," but nowhere is it more strikingly manifested than in the annals of the English Reformation. The work which Henry had begun was completed by his children Edward and Elizabeth. The injunctions of his last will were set aside, his ordinances as to religion were repealed; the heresies which he detested were openly taught and enforced, and all this by the authority of the Royal Supremacy and at the instigation of the men who during his life had been his subservient instruments in infamy from the day that he first severed himself and his people from the unity of Christendom and from the communion of the Apostolic See.

Then there began a fierce war in England against all that Catholics hold sacred, but most of all against the Holy Sacrifice of the Altar, which was regarded by the so-called reformers with a hatred that can only be called satanic. Books full of ribaldry and blasphemy were brought out in which these most august mysteries were held up to public ridicule, and ballads were sung in the alehouses and at the street corners which heaped upon the Holy Sacrifice every possible epithet of hatred and scorn. The churches were desecrated, and the offering of the Divine Liturgy was made a penal offence. Scarcely could Princess Mary, even with the emperor's aid, obtain leave to have what was termed "the idolatrous worship of Baal" celebrated in her private chapel.

Catholic worship was restored for a brief period when

Mary ascended the throne, only once more to be overthrown by her sister Elizabeth. Elizabeth knew well that "it is the Mass that matters," and if she was to succeed in the task she had set herself of rooting out the Catholic religion from the land, she must begin by abolishing the Holy Sacrifice.

So the first symptom of the coming change was seen but a month after her accession, when on Christmas morning she forbade the Bishop of Carlisle to elevate the Host in her presence. When he refused, saying that he could not break the laws of the Catholic Church, even for her Majesty, Elizabeth left the chapel in a rage during the singing of the Gospel. She could not bear to look upon the Lord whom she was about to betray, and a month later a proclamation was issued forbidding throughout England the elevation of the Host. It was the dearest custom of our fathers to gaze upon the sacred Host raised aloft in the hands of the priest; they thought they had not well spent a day on which they had not thus "seen their Maker," as they touchingly expressed it. But henceforth, if Elizabeth had her way, this consolation was to be denied them. The reformers who flocked into England from foreign parts incited the baser people to horrible acts of sacrilege, which were connived at, if not encouraged, by the Government. A cat was hung in Cheapside, clad in sacerdotal vestments, and miscreants stole at night into the churches, and cutting the chains by which the Blessed Sacrament hung in its golden pyx above the altars, trampled beneath their feet the Body of the Lord.

Meanwhile the queen had succeeded in finding a Catholic bishop weak enough to crown her, and on January 15, 1559, she was solemnly consecrated at Westminster with all the ancient rites. She took the solemn oath to maintain the rights and privileges of the Catholic Church intact, and sealed her perjury by a sacrilegious Communion. It was noticed during the service that she openly ridiculed the sacred rite of unction with the ladies of her court.

The last Mass at which she assisted was probably the Mass of the Holy Ghost, which, according to custom, inaugurated her first Parliament, and the first task set before this Parliament was that of abolishing the old religion. The Act of Uniformity was passed in the teeth of the united protests of the Episcopate, and the old order passed away, as it seemed, for ever. Henceforth it was made penal to use the ancient rites of the Catholic Church: the Holy Mass was made an illegal act, the sacraments of Holy Orders, Confirmation, Penance and Unction were abolished, the glorious ceremonies of Holy Week discarded, the ancient language of the Church forbidden and Her most sacred doctrines proscribed. The ancient Church of England met for the last time in solemn conclave, and with united voice protested in Convocation against the destruction of the old religion, solemnly affirming the ancient faith of Christendom in the doctrine of transubstantiation and the supremacy of the Holy See, declaring that to the Church alone it belonged to legislate in matters of faith.

These protests were of course disregarded; the faithful clergy were deprived of their benefices and driven into exile, and the Catholic hierarchy in England perished, for the most part, in the prisons of Elizabeth. Their places were taken by intruders ordained according to the newfangled rite to be "preachers of the word," and not sacrificing priests. To these men the august sacrifice of the altar was an object of intense hatred. Their words, and still more their acts, remain to prove how bitter was the war they waged against the Mass. A tide of sacrilege and profanity flooded the whole land. Everything which had been consecrated to God's service by the piety of our fathers was now defaced and destroyed, or turned to the basest uses. The churches were stripped so bare that the queen actually had to ordain that the Ten Commandments should be painted up on their east walls to show that they were Christian temples. The holy Rood with Mary and John, which stood at the entrance of every chancel, raising men's hearts to the Crucified, was torn down and burnt; and in its place were set up the royal arms with a lion and a dog as supporters.

But it was above all to those objects that were connected with Holy Mass that the greatest contumely was shown. There still exist at Lincoln the returns made by the churchwardens of an archdeaconry of that diocese showing how they had treated the sacred ornaments entrusted to them. To the questions of Archdeacon Aylmer (afterwards Protestant Bishop of London) they protested that all had been defaced. The altar stones were the objects of special detestation. They had been placed as a rule on the pavement that all might trample them under foot (a position in which they may still be seen in many churches), or in other parishes had been turned to still baser uses, such as pigsties, hearthstones, sinks or bridges for cattle. The sacred vestments had been cut up into gowns for the parson's wife and daughters, or used as bed hangings or horse-trappings. The very corporals on which the Body of Christ had lain were used in one place as handkerchiefs, in another as purses, in another as linen for an infant. The pyx, which had held the Blessed Sacrament, was used as a salt cellar, a moneybox or a child's plaything. The holy oils were profaned to grease cart wheels, the sacring bells hung at the necks of cattle, the holy water vat used for milking, the stone stoups for the troughs of swine. The Mass books, the processionals and "all such paltry of the pope's sinful service" were torn in pieces and sold to peddlers "to lap spice in."

In the few cases where some sacred objects had remained unprofaned the church wardens promised that on their return they would utterly deface them.

It must not, however, be supposed that all this was done without indignant protests on the part of the Catholics. In places where the faith was still strong we constantly hear of the sacred ornaments having been "stolen" by the late rector or by the Catholic people; and no doubt in many cases the churchwardens connived in these pious thefts and thus preserved these holy objects for the private use of the ejected and persecuted clergy. It is touching to note that in some places Catholic families had secured the consecrated altars to use as tombs, desiring at once to preserve them from sacrilege and to lay their dead beneath the stones which had been hallowed by the Body of the Lord.

Now began a cruel persecution by which those who still remained faithful were pursued with every ingenuity of cruelty. If they refused to attend the desecrated parish churches and to assist at the new services which had taken the place of the Holy Mass so dear to our fathers, services which had been described by the people of Devon as "no better than a Christmas game," they were liable to heavy fines which impoverished even the rich, and speedily brought the poor to fill the fetid dungeons of every county town. If they attempted in secret to assist at Mass they might at any moment be surprised, seized and thrown into prison.

It was hoped by the queen and her government that as the old clergy died out, the faith would also die out in England, and this would no doubt have been the case — for without priests to offer the sacrifice and to reconcile the people to God, the faith itself cannot long flourish — had it not been for the great man whom God in His mercy chose and raised up to be the Moses of our English Church, William Cardinal Allen. He saw that the persecuted Catholics had urgent need of priests to minister to them, and if they were not provided, the cause of Christ's Church in England was lost. And so he left his old University of Oxford and went into exile for the faith, and at Douay and at Rome he founded famous colleges, in which he trained young men, who flocked to him from Oxford and from Cambridge and from every part of England, and then when they were ordained priests, he sent them back to their country to labor in the Lord's vineyard and to water it, if need be, with their life blood.

For these Seminaries quickly became "Seed-plots of martyrs." The consternation that was caused to Elizabeth and her government when the first seminary priests landed in the country was indeed very great. The persecutors were in despair; they saw instinctively that if Allen's project succeeded, the work to which they had set their hands would never be accomplished. And so, as these young priests, full of apostolic fervor, flocked into the country, the persecution ever grew more fierce, until in 1585 the ever growing structure of the penal laws was crowned by new statutes of almost incredible ferocity. Henceforth any English subject who had received Holy Orders abroad, and who dared to return to England, was by the very fact declared guilty of high treason, and exposed to the frightful penalties reserved for that offence. Henceforth it was only necessary to prove that a man was a Catholic priest to condemn him, and very slight suspicions were often taken as sufficient proofs. To be found with a Breviary or with the holy oils upon him exposed a man to the cruelest and most ignominious of deaths.

And so began the long procession of the Martyrs of the Holy Mass.

"The Douay Registers regularly record the names of the newly ordained priests; the list of 1581 gives the ordination of

52

forty-three priests. Of these fifteen are marked with the letter M, as subsequently martyred. In 1583 the martyrs are ten out of twenty-nine. Next year they are nine out of thirty, and in 1585 ten out of twenty-four. During the last six months of a single year, 1588, there were no less than thirty-three martyrs, twenty-two of whom were priests. Yet the stream of missionaries did not slacken. The report of each fresh martyrdom was celebrated at the college by a Mass of thanksgiving and a solemn Te Deum, and only served to stimulate the zeal and fervor of those who were longing to share the same labors and win the same crown."

But the glories of martyrdom were by no means confined to priests; the same fierce statutes that condemned God's ministers struck at the faithful laymen and women who received them into their houses. It was death to harbor a priest or to relieve his wants, death to receive his absolution, death to assist at his Mass. And so it was often seen that on the great gibbet of Tyburn there were hanging side by side a priest who had offered the sacrifice and a layman who had served his Mass. Nay, indeed, the pious lady who had furnished the altar and embroidered the vestments, here also paid the penalty with her life. These were the Martyrs of the Holy Mass, the victims that were offered on the altar of sacrifice together with the spotless victim of Calvary; these were they who came through great tribulation and washed their robes and made them white in the Blood of the Lamb; these who offered their oblations, the flesh and the blood upon the altar of the Lord their God.

What though the astute tyranny of the persecutor sought to brand them as traitors to their country? Such has been the policy of the persecutors of all time, from those who cried out for the death of the King of Martyrs on the plea that He stirred up the people and was a traitor to Caesar. But their good fame has been amply vindicated in our own day even by the mouths of those who are the children and representatives of their persecutors. An Anglican minister has publicly declared "in the strongest possible terms that the word martyr must be struck out of our vocabulary unless we are prepared to extend its use to these sufferers. They suffered death for their faith," he adds, "though the statute law thought good to call it high treason. It would have been almost as truthful, according to the usual acceptation of the term, to style their offence burglary or poaching."

Nor indeed even in those days were men deceived. There was an aged saint who lived in Rome close to the English College, and whenever he met the students in the street he would salute them with deepest respect, crying: "Salvete flares martyrum — Hail martyr flowers." And before they left for England these young priests were wont to go to beg the blessing of St. Philip, and it was noticed that those whom he lovingly embraced and pressed to his burning heart all gained the crown of martyrdom.

Before we part today let me tell you the story of one of these martyrs of the Holy Mass. It will help you better to realize what manner of men they were, and what were the conflicts they engaged in and the victories they won.

Edmund Gennings was born at Lichfield in the early days of Queen Elizabeth (1567).[12] He was brought up in the new religion, but was remarkable from his childhood for his modesty, docility and piety. He won the heart of his schoolmaster by his zeal for learning, and when a gentleman one day came to Lichfield who wanted a boy to serve him as a page, the master declared that there was no one to be compared to Edmund. This gentleman was a devout Catholic, the uncle of that glorious young martyr, Blessed Thomas Sherwood. He took Edmund with him to London, and before long the boy was eager to be instructed in his master's faith.

He soon proved his fidelity and his zeal, and was entrusted by his master with very difficult commissions in visiting Catholic confessors in the London prisons. But this did not satisfy Edmund's zeal, and his heart burned within him to become a priest of God, to devote his life to the conversion of his country.

And so he found his way to Rheims, where Dr. Allen had been forced to remove his students from Douay, and there he obtained his desire. He advanced rapidly in his studies, but above all in the science of the saints — the love and fear of God. But he was often ill, and at last fell a victim to the scourge of consumption.

---

[12] Edmund Gennings was canonized a saint by Pope Paul VI as one of the 40 English and Welsh martyrs on 25 October 1970.

The physicians declared that his only chance of life was to return to England, to breathe his native air. This grieved him sorely, for he had not yet attained the goal of his desires. He set out, however, in obedience, and arrived at Havre de Grace, where, however, his earnest prayers obtained for him a complete and sudden cure, which appeared miraculous to all who knew him, and he was able to return, full of joy and gratitude, to his studies at college.

His longing for the crown of martyrdom was intense, and when his fellow students talked together of England and of martyrdom he would constantly exclaim: "Vivamus in spe! Vivamus in spe! — Let us live in hope!"

His meditations on the dignity of the priesthood made such an impression on his whole being that it produced a wonderful effect on his very body, a trembling as it were of palsy, which continued with him to his dying day. He was ordained priest at Soissons, March 18, 1590. He was soon sent out to labor in the Lord's vineyard. In the dead of night, after a very stormy passage, he and a companion were landed on a wild and desolate part of the Yorkshire coast, not far from Whitby. Here they nearly fell at once into the hands of the enemy, for they were met by a pursuivant, whose importunate curiosity it was very hard to baffle.

However, they arrived in safety at a Catholic house, where they found a loving and a generous welcome. A good knight (Sir Henry Cholmley), who lived near Whitby, had made his house a place of refuge for priests. They "came there, for the most part, destitute of clothes and money, but were sent away from this charitable house well supplied with both, often in scarlet and satin, with their men and horses, the better to disguise their profession." Here Edmund and his companion found it safest to separate, and bade farewell to each other with mutual embraces and many tears. They were never to meet again in this world.

Our young priest's heart yearned after his family, whom he had left entangled in the Anglican heresy, and he bent his steps forthwith to Lichfield, in the hope of bringing them back to the Catholic faith. But he found to his sorrow that they were all dead, except one young brother, John, who, as he heard, was now in London. He was told that he was not only a Protestant, but that he was leading a wild and sinful life. He longed to save at least this wandering sheep, and he followed him to London and sought for him day and night, but without success. And ever as he sought for him he prayed, offering his life to God for the conversion of this much loved brother.

And then at last, as he walked one day in St. Paul's Churchyard, on his way to say Mass at a Catholic house, he suddenly felt his limbs trembling in an extraordinary manner, and his body bathed in a cold sweat. He thought that perchance it was a warning of danger; but looking round to see if he were pursued, could see no one but a young man in a brown cloak, who was paying no attention to him.

Another day, as he was about to leave London, in despair of finding his brother, the same thing happened to him at almost the same place. He saw again the same young man, and was moved to stop and speak with him.

He soon discovered that it was indeed his brother, but did not at once make himself known. "Where is thy brother Edmund?" he asked him. The youth replied that he had become a Papist and, as he heard, a priest; that he was abroad, and if he ventured to come back he would assuredly be hanged. After a time Father Edmund ventured to disclose himself to his brother, but he could make no impression on his heart, for the young man was wholly given up to the pleasures and vanities of the world. After many conversations the priest had the pain of seeing that his toil was fruitless, and he determined to leave London. But though he knew it not, God had accepted his sacrifice, and in him the old truth was once more to be made manifest: "Except a corn of wheat fall into the earth and die, it abideth alone, but if it die, it bringeth forth much fruit."(John 12: 24-25)

A day or two before he was to leave London, Edmund met a brother priest in Holborn and they agreed to say their Matins together and to say Mass the following morning at the house of Mr. Swithun Wells, a devout Catholic who lived in Grays Inn Fields.

It was the Octave of All Saints, and as Father Gennings was offering the adorable sacrifice in an upper room a violent knocking was heard at the house doors, and the infamous Topcliffe, most notorious of priest catchers, burst into the house at the head of a troop of pursuivants. The gentlemen who were present stood at the door of the Oratory with their drawn swords, and when Topcliffe, raging like a lion, sought to burst through them, one of them hurled him downstairs. They told him if he would wait till the Sacrifice was completed they would yield themselves up to him without resistance; but they would give their lives rather than allow the adorable mysteries to be profaned. And so they knelt with drawn swords until the awful rite was finished, and then yielded themselves up like lambs to the slaughter. The holy priest was torn from the altar still clad in his sacred vestments, and thus led through the streets at the head of the little procession of prisoners, followed by a mocking crowd who hurled stones and mud at them. They were of course all condemned to die, including their host, who had not been at home at the time of the occurrence but had been arrested subsequently.

When Swithun Wells came home to find his house in possession of the pursuivants and his family in prison he went to the judge to ask what it all meant. The judge said to him: "I suppose you went away because you did not approve of all this?" "Oh, no, indeed," replied the martyr. "I give thanks to God that my house was so highly honored by having so divine a sacrifice offered therein, and I only wish that I had been present." "Well," said the judge to him, "if you were not present at the feast, you shall taste of the sauce," and he was joined to the blessed company of the martyrs. They might all have saved their lives by consenting to attend the Protestant service, but this they steadily refused to do. Father Edmund's constancy so enraged the judges that they had him thrust into a dark hole within the prison. Here he remained absorbed in prayer, without any food for five days. The day of martyrdom was Friday, December 10. When drawn to the place of execution, which was opposite the house where the Mass had been celebrated, the holy priest saluted the gibbet in the words of St. Andrew: "O good cross, long desired and now prepared for me, much has my heart desired thee, and now joyful and secure I come to thee. Receive me, I beseech thee, as a disciple of Him who suffered on the cross."

When urged by Topcliffe to confess his treason, he cried aloud: "If to return into England a priest or to say Mass be popish treason, I acknowledge myself guilty of these things, not with sorrow but with joy; and if they were to do again, I would by God's permission and assistance accomplish the same at the hazard of a thousand lives." This made Topcliffe so angry that he had the rope cut immediately, and the martyr fell scarcely stunned and stood with eyes raised to heaven till the hangman began the work of butchery. As he cried out in his pain, old Mr. Wells, who stood by waiting for his turn, exclaimed: "Alas! sweet soul, thy pain is great indeed, but almost past. Pray for me now, most holy saint, that mine may come." And when his heart was already in the hangman's hand, the martyr was distinctly heard to whisper: "Holy Gregory, pray for me." At this the hangman cried out with an oath: "See the vile papist: his heart is in my hand, and yet Gregory is in his mouth." And indeed there was never perhaps a testimony more striking and more touching to the traditional love which England bore to her Pope-Apostle than this last cry of the dying priest who was giving his life for the Holy Mass.

And thus this young man (he was but twenty-four years old) offered to God the supreme sacrifice of love, and went to join the company of His saints.

And now mark how the God of love accepted the sacrifice of His servant.

The young brother, far from bewailing the martyr's cruel death, rather rejoiced in it, as it rid him of his pious importunities. But about ten days after the martyrdom, he went home one night, after a day spent in riotous pleasure, and going to his room, fell into a fit of deep melancholy. The contrast between his brother's holy life and death and his own loose way of living came home to him as it had never done before, and he felt his heart pierced with grief and remorse.

And then he saw his brother's, form, glorified and beautiful beyond expression, and radiant with celestial light, and at this vision he fell on his knees and began to weep and pray for God's assistance. And then, of a sudden, his soul was illuminated, and he saw the truth. Nor did he rise before he had made a vow to forsake kindred and country to embrace the faith for which his brother died; and this vow he made haste to fulfill.

"The blood of the martyrs is the seed of the Church." This wild young man became a Catholic, a priest, and a religious; and as Father John Gennings he restored the English Province of the Franciscan Order, and thus became the spiritual father of many martyrs. Such is the simple story of one of these martyrs of the Holy Mass. Shall we not love that sacrifice for which men like this so gladly gave their lives?

We read of our persecuted forefathers that nothing was so dear to them as this adorable sacrifice. When the Jesuit Father Persons went over to England in 1580 he was astonished at the fervor of the people. "It fills me with amazement," he wrote, "when I behold and reflect upon the devotion which Catholics in England show by their gestures and behavior at Mass; for they are overpowered by such a sense of awe and reverence that when they hear the name of the pope pronounced in the Office they beat their breasts, and when the Lord's Body is elevated they weep so abundantly as to draw tears even from my dry and parched eyes." Indeed the Elizabethan persecution brought about an immense increase of life and fervor among the Catholics of the realm. Devotion to the Vicar of Christ, that unfailing test of a true Catholic spirit, had taken the place of the old indifference, and the Holy Sacrifice of the Mass had become the consolation of their lives. The people would entreat the priests, who came at the risk of their lives to offer the Holy Sacrifice, to prolong the celebration as much as possible in order the better to satisfy their devotion; and they would gladly go long and perilous journeys at night and on foot in order to assist at Holy Mass in some ancient manor house or secluded cottage. A layman who spent three years in England in the very height of the persecution tells us that during the whole time never a day passed that he had not the consolation of hearing Mass, and that on Sundays three or four Masses would be offered in the same house. When we remember the constant dangers which beset both celebrant and assistants we can realize how great was the devotion which braved these perils.

We, my brethren, who are the children of the martyrs, have the treasure of the Holy Mass constantly at our disposal; we have to run no risks, to fear no dangers, in assisting at these adorable mysteries day by day. Are we thankful enough for the grace thus lavishly bestowed upon us? Do we use the Mass as we should: eagerly, thankfully, gratefully? Surely we should never allow a day to pass on which by our own fault we have not assisted at this divine sacrifice! Rather let us cherish it as our most inestimable privilege, rejoicing if we are able frequently to assist at the sacrifice, doing all in our power to increase these opportunities both for ourselves and for others. Let us never allow sloth or worldly cares to rob us of our daily Mass! Nay, let us love the Altar of God, counting it our glory to add to its material beauty, spending and being spent in the service of the sanctuary. Happy indeed are we if we are able to make sacrifices for the adornment of God's altar, happier still if we are allowed to give to God a priest who may offer day by day this adorable sacrifice.

Those of you to whom God has given sons, pray that you may be counted worthy to give them back to Him as priests. And those who have not this blessing may at least by their generous alms help to train for the altar some poor lad to whom our divine Lord has given the immense grace of a sacerdotal vocation. Oh, how happy are those who are thus enabled to multiply the offering of the Holy Sacrifice; great will be their blessings here on earth, and greater yet their eternal reward in heaven.

And finally, my brethren, let us entreat the mercy of God, that the adorable sacrifice of the altar may be restored to every ancient cathedral and parish church throughout the land. They were raised, these glorious temples, by the piety of our fathers for the celebration of these divine mysteries. They now stand desolate, profaned to alien and heretic uses. Ah, if we might live to see Holy Mass sung once more in Canterbury or Durham or Gloucester, surely then would we gladly sing our *Nunc Dimittis*![13]

"But they have violated God's holy places, they have defiled His sanctuaries," and —terrible thought— "He was profaned in the midst of them." (Ez 22:26) Let us pray and do penance and entreat the aid of our martyrs, that God would in His mercy rebuild the fallen altars and make glad the desolate places.

"Our fathers have sinned and done evil in the sight of the Lord God, forsaking Him; they have turned away their faces from

---

[13] The *Nunc Dimmittis* is Simeon's canticle: "Now thou dost dismiss thy servant, O Lord . . ."

the tabernacle of the Lord, and turned their backs. They have put out their lamps, and have not burnt incense, nor offered holocaust in the sanctuary . . . and they endeavor to cast us out of the possession which Thou hast delivered to us" (2 Par. 29: 6-8).

But surely God, for His martyrs' sake, "hath not forsaken us, but hath extended His mercy upon us to give us life, and to set up the house of our God, and to rebuild the desolations thereof" (1Esdras 9:9).

IV

The Martyrs the Glory of England

Wednesday (morning), May 4, 1904

"Let us now praise men of renown and our fathers in their generation. Rich men in virtue, living at peace in their houses, men of mercy whose godly deeds have not failed, good things continue with their seed, their posterity are a holy inheritance, and their seed bath stood in the covenants; their seed and their glory shall not be forsaken. Their bodies are buried in peace, and their name liveth unto generation and generation. Let the people show forth their wisdom and let the Church declare their praise."
—*Ecclus 44: 1, 6, 10-15*

Love for our native country is implanted in our breasts by God; it grows with our growth as naturally as does our love for the parents from whom we derive our life. Patriotism is a natural virtue, and a man who has no love for the land that gave him birth and nurtured him would be a monster only to be compared with those evil men whom the Apostle describes as "without natural affection."

And as we love our country, so we rejoice in its glory and sorrow in its misfortunes. Its very name brings a light to our eyes and a glow to our cheeks. When we are absent from it for a time, we return to its shores with delight; it gladdens our ears to hear once more the familiar tongue which we learned unconsciously at our mother's knee, and we feel that, though other lands have their advantages, yet for us there is no place like home. And who can describe the yearning love that fills the exile's heart for the dear shores of his native land? It echoes like a refrain through their words and thoughts and sighs; the longer they live away from it the deeper does its dear name print its impress on their hearts, the more fervent grow the prayers for its prosperity and peace, the more intense the longing to see its shores once more.

My sisters, forgive me if I have touched a painful chord. Some of you know well the love and longing of the exile's heart, and yet to the religious there is no such thing as exile, for Jesus only is the portion of his inheritance and his lot. Still, though we know this well, we cannot but love most deeply the land that gave us birth.

And we Englishmen, my brethren, rejoice in our native land: this England of ours so fair and free, so great and glorious, so strong, so beautiful; how should we not love it? And with our love is mingled pride in its glories and sorrows in its loss.

We are Catholics first of all, for we belong to Christ and then to our native land. God forbid that we should be among those who boast that they are Englishmen first and Christians next! No, we are Christ's; we belong, and it is our greatest glory to belong, to the great family of Christ's Holy Church, Catholic, Apostolic and Roman. This Church is as wide as the love of Christ; she knows no human barriers, no geographical limits, no boundaries of continent or sea; she embraces the human race, the children of our father Adam, and rising above the earth even to the very throne of God in heaven claims as her own the star-crowned Queen of Saints and all her blessed subjects, yes, and the suffering holy souls who yet sigh in the dim penitential realm of purgatory. And therefore, being children of the Catholic Church, our natural patriotism for our native land is raised to a higher level, is supernaturalized, so to speak, is transformed in the light of faith.

We look upon this England of ours,

> "This royal throne of kings, this sceptred isle,
> This earth of majesty, this seat of Mars,
> This other Eden, demi-paradise ... .
> This precious stone, set in the silver sea . .
> This land of such dear souls, this dear, dear land"

not with less love than do our fellow-countrymen, but with a different kind of love, with a deeper, higher, truer love, with a love that is as distinct from the foolish noisy chauvinism of the street and the music hall as was the love of a St. Monica or a St. Felicitas for her children from the mere animal instinct of a tigress for her whelps.

We look at our dear country with mingled joy and sorrow. We see her great and glorious, feared and envied by other nations, rich and prosperous and powerful, but this gives us little joy. For with the light that faith bestows we see how vain and transitory is all this glory; we see that it is not for a moment to be compared to the glory that is alone of value in the sight of God and His holy angels, the glory that the world despises and condemns, of a country united in the one true faith, loyal to Christ and to His Vicar, a garden of saints and a home of virtue and peace. When we weigh the glories of England in the balance of the sanctuary, we are forced to confess that those things which dazzled our eyes and attracted our admiration at first are indeed as nothing compared with the blessings of the faith and the glory of Christian unity. We learn to see that if the humiliation of our dearest country before her foes, and her fall from her proud place among the nations were a necessary condition of her return to the fold of Christ, we ought not for a moment to hesitate as to which we should desire and pray for. Do not misunderstand me. Every true patriotic heart must instinctively cry a "God forbid" at the thought of such a choice being necessary; still, I repeat, were it really to prove true that England's return to the unity of Christendom should depend, in the mysterious counsels of God, on her humiliation in worldly glory, we ought not to shrink from the condition, deeply though it would pierce our hearts, or desire her worldly prosperity at the cost of the salvation of her sons.

Some cruel dilemma of this kind was actually put before our blessed martyrs in the sixteenth century. On the one hand they saw their sovereign going on his headlong way and dragging the nation after him into schism and heresy. On the other hand they fixed their eyes on the Catholic sovereigns of Europe, and asked themselves if it were not better that their country should be invaded by foreigners, and this cruel tyranny of the persecutor be put a stop to, and England preserved or restored to the unity of the Church. As a matter of fact, we know that they never had actually the practical choice presented to them but once. But long years before the Spanish Armada invaded our coasts, Blessed John Fisher had urged the emperor, through his ambassador, to use force, since all other means had failed to stop the intolerable tyranny of Henry VIII. Who shall dare to blame the holy prelate? Who question the purity of his patriotism? Who loved our England more passionately than he did? Nay, it was because he loved her so deeply that he felt anything would be tolerable rather than to see her dragged into the abyss of heresy and cut off from the communion of Christ's Church.

In the time of the Armada circumstances had changed. The evil was done, and it was very doubtful if force would provide any remedy. The Catholics of England too had good reason to doubt the purity of the motives of the monarch who invaded their shores with the avowed object of restoring the Catholic faith in their midst. They felt on the one hand that the experiment of conversion by force had already been tried when Philip of Spain ruled over England, and had signally failed, and on the other, that here there was much unavowed secular ambition masked under the fair cloak of zeal for the Church of Christ. They therefore rallied round their Protestant queen in the hour of danger; and again who shall blame their choice?

Indeed, the loyalty of our persecuted forefathers has ever been one of the most astonishing phenomena of English history. How were they rewarded for their patriotic services and their patriotic sacrifices under the Armada? Alas! By a still fiercer persecution than that under which they had already groaned. In the last six months of the Armada year (1588) no less than thirty-two martyrs suffered, and the land was deluged with their blood. Among these heroic and innocent victims twenty-one were priests, ten laymen, and one was a heroic lady, who gladly gave her life for having rescued a priest from the clutches of the persecutors.

If we love our country, then, we shall estimate her glories in the balance of the sanctuary. And then indeed we shall see and understand that it is not her mighty and unvanquished navy, not her far-spreading and fruitful dominions, not the splendor of her rule nor the wisdom of her constitution, not these nor any other worldly advantage, that make her glorious in the eyes of God, but that the true glory of, England are the blessed saints whom she has nurtured in her bosom, those innocent, meek and humble souls whose name the world hardly knows; those saintly bishops, those royal virgins, those countless monks and nuns, and above all that white-robed army of martyrs who have poured out their blood like water for the name of Christ and the cause of His Church.

Yes, my brethren, the land is dyed in blood! In the eyes of the blessed angels it must glow crimson of hue like a blood red rose upon the heart of God! From north to south, from east to west, from Newcastle to Launceston, from Norwich to Anglesea it has been bathed in the purest blood that ever flowed from human hearts. In every busy market town the drops of that blood are seen; the roads and lanes and fields are bathed in it, for they have been trodden down by many a martyr's feet. It glows in the hearts of our English wild flowers; the red soil of Devon speaks eloquently of it, the crumbling walls of our abbey ruins and of many an ancient manor house are tinged with it, the streets of this London of ours are blazoned with its hues. This sacred spot where we stand, unworthy that we are to tread ground so holy, is dyed deep as the Savior's purple robe, and all around us beneath the sod, pressed daily by thousands of hurrying, unconscious feet, lie the sacred relics of the blessed martyrs of England whose souls are in the hands of God.

These to the eyes of faith are the true glory of our land. We grieve over the apostasy of our people, over the self-willed obstinacy of our sovereigns who robbed the country of its faith, and desolated the land that rejoiced to be called the Dowry of Mary. But there is comfort amid the pain, and the greater and the more widespread the ruin, the purer and, brighter the glory of those who remained faithful until death.

"This noble band," says the papal beatification, "lacks neither fullness of numbers nor grade of honor. It is adorned with the splendor of the Roman purple, it is dignified by venerable bishops, it comprises magnanimous priests both secular and regular; the invincible firmness of the weaker sex is also there." Yes, indeed, in the day of trial England was not sparing of her best and purest blood. Had you asked the tyrant himself in the days of his Catholic fervor who was the most saintly and venerable bishop of his dominions, he would have replied without hesitation, "Fisher of

Rochester." Had you inquired who was the most eminent layman, he would have answered that of all the glories of his court none was so brilliant, none so illustrious, as Thomas More, the man whom he most delighted to honor. Had you asked who was the most saintly woman, the king would have replied (we have the assurance of her son, Cardinal Pole, for it): "Margaret, Countess of Salisbury, is she whom I most venerate in all my realm." Had you gone about this London, and asked in which of the numerous monasteries there dwelt the most fervent religious, you would have been directed as by one voice to the London Charterhouse. Had you answered that you wanted not men of contemplation alone, but apostolic preachers and enlightened directors, the first passerby would have said: "Go to the Observant Franciscans." Had you wished to visit one of the glorious Benedictine monasteries, which in those happy days covered the face of the country, and hesitated as to where you would find the most edifying observance, the most enlightened learning, the most holy examples, you would doubtless have been guided to the famous Sanctuary of Glastonbury, and to its abbot, Dom Richard Whiting.

Could an angel have opened the roll of the future before the eyes of Henry Tudor while he was yet young, and let him read therein that he was destined to shed the blood of all these servants of God, solely for their loyalty to the Apostolic See, we may well believe that he would have started back in horror, crying like Hazael the Syrian: "Is thy servant a dog, that he should do this thing?"(4 Kings 8:13) But we know how the indulgence of one fatal passion brought him to do all this, and more than this. Yes; for today we celebrate with Holy Mass and hymns of thanksgiving the memory of those blessed ones who gave their lives for the rights of the Apostolic See and the truth of the orthodox faith.

And with them we join the memory of one-and-twenty blessed priests and four glorious laymen who shed their blood for the same sacred cause under Elizabeth. There are many more indeed, hundreds more, whose cause was the same, and whose glory in heaven is no doubt the same, but who we are not yet permitted publicly to venerate and to invoke.

But here at Tyburn, on this fourth of May, let us thank God for those who have poured out their blood. For the protomartyrs, who upon this very day witnessed a good confession; for Edward Campion, once the pride of Oxford, and now one of the brightest stars in the great constellation of the saints of the company of Jesus; for Alexander Bryant, that youth of angelic face and seraphic love; for Thomas Sherwood, so small in stature, yet so brave of heart; for Thomas Cottam, of the tender conscience and the steadfast soul; for Ford and Johnson and Filby and all the rest, with their dear familiar English names, their English faces, and their English hearts.

Yes, indeed, these are the true glories of our England, did she but know it! Brethren, we offer the sacrifice today on the spot where they offered their own last sacrifice, that their glory may be made known in the land and that the children of those that afflicted them may come to them and worship the ground under their feet.

Tyburn's wrongs are long forgiven, unforgotten is the pain;
Time can never dim the traces of the cruel blood-red stain;
And the martyrs' cry for vengeance rises up before Thy throne,
'Save the land we love so well, Lord; claim its children for Thine own.'

V

The Martyrs our hope for the Conversion of England

Wednesday, May 4, at Benediction

"Converte Domine captivitatem nostram sicut torrens in Austro. Qui seminant in lacrymis, in exultatione metent. Euntes ibant et flebant, mittentes semina sua. Venientes autem venient cum exultatione, portantes manipulos suos — Turn again our captivity, O Lord, as a stream in the south; those who sow in tears shall reap in joy. Going they went and wept, casting their seeds. But coming they shall come with joyfulness bearing their sheaves." — Ps. 125: 4-7

WE meet today, my brethren, upon a great anniversary: the day which commemorates the martyrdom of those glorious servants of God who were drawn to this place along the Oxford Road from Newgate and from the Tower, drawn on hurdles beyond the gates of the city, to this Calvary of England's Church, that they might give the supreme witness of love to England's ancient faith.

It was on this day that the protomartyrs of Tyburn began the long procession which makes these crowded streets to the eye of faith a veritable *Via Dolorosa*.[14] For 150 years that procession went on which was headed today by the white-robed monks of the Charterhouse, and had its climax, as was fitting, in the stately form of a great Christian bishop. As in our ecclesiastical processions the religious come first, then follow the secular clergy, and at the end the pontiff; so in this great procession of the Tyburn martyrs.

---

[14] Via Dolorosa - Sorrowful Way

It was a procession like that which inaugurates some stately function, some pontifical High Mass in one of the great cathedrals of Christendom. But here the procession is still more wondrous, still more sublime; for each figure that takes part in it is himself about to offer the sacrifice, is himself both victim and priest. And so they pass before us in triumphal array with songs of victory on their lips and the light of heaven in their eyes. They pass, the humble sons of Benedict, Bruno, Francis and Ignatius, who have left their cloisters to swell the long drawn ranks; they pass, those bright young forms from Douay, Rome and Valladolid, the messengers who came to bring us the Gospel of peace, with their angelic faces and their joyous hymns. They pass, those young brave laymen, who bear England's proudest names, but who held it greater glory to share the shame of the cross with their fathers in the faith. They pass those heroic women who ministered to God's servants as did the sisters of Bethany to their divine Master, and who in recompense of their devotion have obtained that great reward for which they prayed. Lastly, in his purple robes, passes the white-haired pontiff, the successor of St. Patrick, the glory of two kingdoms, blessing as he goes.[15]

They bear in their hands the palm of victory; their heads are encircled with the aureole of martyrdom. And now that they stand before the throne of heaven, what is the prayer which springs from the lips of all; what is the strain they join in raising to the martyrs' King? "In convertendo Dominus captivitatem Sion; facti sumus sicut consolati; tunc repletum est gaudio os nostrum, et lingua nostra exultatione — When the Lord turned again the captivity of Sion, then were we filled with consolation. . . . Turn again our captivity, O Lord, as a stream in the south. They that sow in tears shall surely reap in joy. Lord, we have gone on our way weeping, casting good seed; oh, hasten the time when we may come again with joy, bearing our sheaves with us!" (see Ps.125)

---

[15] The Venerable Oliver Plunket, Archbishop of Armagh, the last martyr of Tyburn (canonized by Pope Paul VI on 10 December 1975).

"Jesus, convert England; Jesus, have mercy on this country." The dying prayer of one of the martyrs of Tyburn was in truth the motive power of the lives of all of them. What brought them back to England to suffer and to die? What but the love of their country or rather the love of Christ? It was because they loved their country so dearly that they longed to do their utmost to win back some of her erring children into the fold of Peter. It was because they loved Christ so truly that they longed to satisfy this thirst for souls.

There was in the sixteenth century a nun in Spain who heard the sad story of the fearful ravages which heresy was causing in Germany and France and England — how men were profaning the sanctuaries of God and trampling His sacraments under their feet and leading away the ignorant by thousands into soul-destroying error. And as she listened, her heart burnt within her and she longed to do something to snatch these souls from death. She seemed to see them falling into hell as the leaves drift from the trees in autumn, and her soul was pierced with anguish at the sight. She cried: "Behold, O eternal Father, how the souls for which Thy Son suffered such grievous torments to save, are being lost! How can you endure that heretics should despise those holy sacraments, and demolish the churches where Thy Son dwelt? Has He not abundantly overpaid for Adam's sin? Suffer not this, O my Emperor? May your Majesty at last be appeased, look not on our sins, but on your most holy Son who redeemed us, and on His merits and those of His glorious mother and on so many saints and martyrs who suffered death for you. O eternal Father, hear one who would lose a thousand honors and a thousand lives for you. Not for our sakes, O Lord, as we deserve it not, but for the Blood of your Son and for His merits have pity on the souls that perish; Lord, give me souls, give me souls!"

So she prayed; nor was she contented with prayer alone. She grieved that she was not a man that she might go forth and preach to the souls that sit in darkness and in the shadow of death; she longed to shed her blood for them, but since this could not be, she did what she could. She reformed the ancient order to which she belonged, restoring it to its primitive fervor and founded (though without money and without human aid) more than thirty monasteries in which her daughters might pray and do penance until the end of time for the salvation of souls. She used to say to them: "What does it matter though we stay in purgatory to the day of judgment if but one soul be saved by our prayers?"

She realized the value of a soul; that its value was that of the price which had been paid for it, the value of the Precious Blood of Jesus. And so she prayed unceasingly and offered up to God the sweet odor of a mortified life for the souls of men. She used to say that if our Lord had said to her what He said to St. Thomas of Aquinas, " What reward wilt thou have of Me?" she would have replied, "Da mihi animas — Lord, give me souls." And so it was when St. Teresa lay down to die at Alba del Tormes; it was revealed to a great servant of God that this poor nun had converted to God more souls than even the great apostle of the Indies, St. Francis Xavier, who baptized hundreds of thousands with his own hand.

Such is the power of prayer and sacrifice over the heart of God. And when we look at our martyrs, who beneath the altar of God in heaven continually cry out: "O Lord, avenge the blood of Thy servants which hath been shed," who continually offer before the throne the incense of their supplication and the merits of their blood, surely then our hearts are filled with hope. It can never be that such prayer should not be heard, never be that such pure blood should have been poured out in vain! Yes, the martyrs are our hope for the conversion of England.

We saw yesterday how these heroic men threw themselves into the breach and led the forlorn hope when the cause of God's Church in England seemed lost and hopeless. We saw those ardent young men flock to the Seminaries in Flanders, Spain and Italy to prepare for the priestly office and the martyr's palm. And to their aid there came eager volunteers from the great religious orders, none of which were willing to be deprived of a share in an enterprise so glorious and so sacred.

First of the ancient orders came, as was their right, the sons of St. Benedict; they who centuries before had won the glorious title of England's apostles, and by an unparalleled series of bloodless victories had subdued the land to the sweet yoke of Christ. There followed close behind them the sons of Francis,

Dominic and Teresa, bringing to the work the old heroic spirit of self-sacrificing love, apostolic zeal and fruitful penance, which had transformed the face of Italy and Spain, and given martyrs to the Church in eastern lands. And with them were conspicuous the sons of the soldier-saint of Loyola, ever to the front where the danger is greatest, counting their lives as worthless for the love of souls. One high aim fired the souls of all, one prayer was ever on their lips, one end ever before their eyes — the conversion of England to the Catholic faith.

And here again I will tell you the story of one of them, but one of many, yet typical of all.

Henry Heath was born of Protestant parents at Peterborough in the last year of the sixteenth century. He became a scholar at Corpus Christi College, Cambridge, and was remarkable for his love of study. He would rise at two in the morning in order to get to his books. His piety was great, and though he was not a Catholic, he was an earnest seeker after truth. After taking his degree he became librarian of his college, and thus the custodian of the splendid collection of manuscripts, spoils from the ancient monastic libraries, which had happily escaped destruction, and were, as they still are, preserved at the college. His zeal for truth led him to a close examination of the religious controversies of the day, and he read the chief writers on either side. To his astonishment he discovered that the Anglican controversialists were dishonest and untrustworthy in their quotations from the Fathers, and on turning to these he found that they knew nothing of the doctrines in which he had been reared. By means of his patristic studies his eyes were opened to the truth, and his soul illumined by the grace of God. The treasure that he had found he sought to share with others, and he made known to the little band of college friends who had gathered round him his wonderful discovery. Four of them became Catholics, and subsequently entered religion.

He soon found himself in danger of arrest, and had to leave the University. Arrived in London, he sought for a priest to reconcile him to God. But at first he only met with rebuffs. In those sad days, when spies and false brethren were everywhere to be found, Catholics had to use the greatest circumspection in making known to strangers the retreats where their priests were hidden. In this perplexity the young man remembered to have read how Catholics in their difficulties had recourse to our Blessed Lady, and so for the first time he turned to the Mother of God and implored her aid, promising that he would in return dedicate himself to her service. Almost immediately after this he met a Catholic gentleman, who had before repulsed him, and found that he was completely changed. He now most kindly offered to take him to a priest, and thus the young convert made his confession and was received into the Church.

He then went over to Douay, and studied for awhile in the famous college founded by Cardinal Allen. There he found that John Gennings, the brother of the martyr whose conversion I recounted to you yesterday, had lately established in the town a convent of Franciscan friars, which was to be the nucleus of the restored English Province of the Order. Heath was profoundly impressed by what he saw of the life of these friars, their poverty, penance and apostolic fervor, and he soon began to desire to join them. This, after some delay imposed by the prudence of his confessor, he was allowed to do, and Father Gennings received him into the Order of St. Francis, under the name of Paul of St. Magdalen. He soon became a model of religious observance, even for the most perfect. He was not content with the austerities of the rule, but stripped himself of the barest necessities of life. He fasted four or five days in the week on a little dry bread, and wore continually a rough hairshirt and an iron chain beneath his habit. He snatched a few hours' sleep on the bare boards of his cell, but frequently spent the whole night in prayer. Above all, he was a pattern of obedience, gentleness and meekness. In time he became a profound and brilliant theologian, and for many years taught scholastic theology to the students of his province. But his zeal for perfection increased step by step with his learning. As with most truly mortified interior souls his penance was rewarded by abundant consolations, and he was almost constantly inundated with spiritual joy. He has left behind him a precious little book of spiritual instructions, which has been often reprinted, and has helped many souls to make good progress on the thorny paths of perfection.

But the two most striking characteristics of this favored

soul were his love for the Blessed Virgin and his burning thirst for martyrdom.

He was truly a child of Mary. As we have seen, he owed to her intercession his reception into the Catholic Church. When a deadly fever raged in his community at Douay he obtained his own cure and that of his brethren from her who is the Comforter of the afflicted and the Health of the sick. And when his heart was sore for his aged father, who persisted in heresy, he recommended him to the same Blessed Mother. And lo! One day the old man knocked at the convent door. He had come over of his own accord from England to seek admission into the Catholic fold, and he ended his days in peace as a humble lay-brother in his son's convent. Father Heath had then good reason for his loving confidence in this Help of Christians; and so when the crown of martyrdom, for which he daily sighed, seemed to be for ever beyond his grasp, it was to the blessed Queen of Martyrs that he turned with unfailing trust, and as we shall see, it was through her intervention that he obtained his desire.

In 1641 he received the news that his dearest friend and brother religious, Father Coleman, lay in Newgate with six companions under sentence of death. His heart was at once inflamed with a vehement desire to share their happiness. He wrote to the confessors a glowing letter of congratulation, in which he cried: "Alas, how great is my unhappiness that I am not permitted to come to you, that I might be partaker of your chains, and offer myself to be consumed with that ardent desire of Jesus Christ which in your trials has made you so constant and victorious over human fears! ... . O good Jesus, what crime am I guilty of, that I am not to be allowed to join your company? For there is nothing in the world that I desire more, nor is it possible that anything can satisfy me so long as I am separated from you."

Meanwhile this generous heart knew no rest. He threw himself at the feet of his superiors, imploring them to allow him to go to England. He told them that he had lost his peace of mind, that he could not rest at night, and that as he lay awake it seemed to him continually as if the hangman were putting the rope round his neck. But though moved at his fervor, the superiors did not see their way to granting his prayer, since his presence was greatly needed at Douay. He then entreated to be allowed to make a pilgrimage to the famous shrine of our Lady of Montaigu, near Louvain, and this he easily obtained.

He was confident that Mary would obtain for him this much desired grace. He addressed her in burning words: "If this be granted me," he prayed, "thou wilt see with what willingness and alacrity I shall give my bare back to be placed upon burning coals, with what joy I shall drink the most bitter chalice, with what glad and eager gaze I shall look on that much desired knife, even while it transfixes me: that knife which will deliver me from this wearisome and miserable prison, and introduce me to the longed for presence of thy dearest Son, Jesus, where, in company with thee, I shall dwell for ever. Amen. Quick, quick, quick!"

He passed the night before the miraculous image, where so many suppliants have knelt and have obtained what they came to seek. But surely none ever came with such a prayer as his! And he was heard. On his return the difficulties melted away; his superiors were unable longer to resist his pleading, and he obtained the permission he sought.

Father Paul appeared transfigured on receiving their answer; heaven had begun already in his soul. He spoke with rapture of the glory of the martyrs, as though he was already sharing it, and his every look, word and act betrayed the intensity of his interior peace and joy.

He lost no time in setting out, going in his religious habit, barefoot and without money, as his rule prescribed. At Dunkirk he had his friar's gown made into a secular dress, and he obtained from the charity of a stranger his passage to Dover. He begged his way to London, and arrived there poor and needy, without money and destitute of all help, after a day's walk of forty miles. He lay down to sleep on a doorstep, where he was found by the master of the house and given into custody. Some Catholic writings were found on him, and he was carried off to prison. He boldly confessed his priesthood, and said that he had come to England to save souls from the servitude of the devil, and to convert them from heresy. Sentence was speedily pronounced, upon which he said: "I give thanks to this honorable court for the singular favor they have done me, and now I am going to die for Christ."

In prison he was confined with criminals, but not content with this ignominy, he asked to be loaded with chains. He heard the confessions of the Catholics, who flocked to him, and administered Holy Communion to more than five hundred of the faithful.

From his dungeon he wrote to his superior: "What other thing can I desire than to suffer with Christ, to be reproached with Christ, to die a thousand deaths that I may live for ever with Christ. ... Let then the executioners come; let them tear my body in pieces; let them gnaw my flesh with their teeth; let them pierce me through and through and grind me to dust. For I know, I know full well, how profitable it will be for me to die for Christ." These wonderful words remind us of the aged St. Ignatius of Antioch, desiring to be ground to dust in the jaws of the lions.

When the longed for day of his death came, he was filled with an inexpressible joy. To some one who wondered at this, he beautifully replied: "I never doubted that my most merciful God would grant a special sweetness to him who laid down his life for justice and the defense of the faith, but I could not possibly have conceived anything so excessive as the joy I now experience, and which so overwhelms and melts my soul that I can scarcely bear it."

And so he was drawn to Tyburn, reciting the *Nunc Dimittis* on the way, and devoutly invoking the holy name of Jesus. With the rope round his neck he recited the hymn, *Martyr Dei qui unicum*, in honor of the Pope Anicetus, whose feast it was. And then he murmured his last prayer, that prayer which echoes still in the hearts of all that love our country: "Jesus, convert England. O England, be converted to the Lord thy God." And so he died most sweetly, even as he breathed forth his last prayer for the country that he loved.

Jesus, convert England. It is the prayer of our hearts today. It has been the prayer of generations of faithful Catholics since the martyr died. "Te insulae expectabunt et nomen tuum invocabunt, parce Domine populo tuo, et ne des hereditatem tuam in opprobrium. — Yes, O Lord, the islands shall wait for Thee, and shall invoke Thy name. Spare, O Lord, spare Thy people, and give not Thy heritage to reproach." (Joel 2:17) O God of mercy and of truth, incline the hearts of the children to their Father. May they look to the Rock from which they have been hewn. "Renew Thy signs and work new miracles; glorify Thy hand and Thy right arm; hasten the time and remember the end, that they may declare Thy wonderful works. Have mercy on Jerusalem, the city which Thou hast sanctified, the city of Thy rest; reward them that patiently wait for Thee, that Thy prophet may be found faithful, and hear the prayers of Thy servants" (Ecclus 36:6-7, 10, 15,18).

My brethren, when we look around us today and compare this sanctuary of Tyburn with the Tyburn of 200 years ago, we are filled with thankfulness and hope. "God has done great things for us already whereof we rejoice."

There are signs of a glad change coming over the length and breadth of the land. Conversions were never perhaps more frequent, and a whole section of the Anglican Church seems to be turning its eyes with longing towards the Mother and Mistress of all churches; many and many a soul, wearied with the jarring discords of warring sects and incompatible creeds, turns a wistful gaze towards the one Church that dares to speak with the infallible authority of God, the one religion in which men know what they believe and why they believe it.

We have emerged from the Catacombs. The Church in all her divine beauty stands forth boldly in the midst of this Protestant land. She is protected by the children of her persecutors, and multitudes begin to be attracted by the heavenly sweetness of her aspect and the sublime grandeur of her unchangeable doctrines. She holds out to our people the priceless gifts of truth, and many hands are stretched out to grasp them.

And as we see all this, our hearts are filled with thoughts such as inspired the prophet's song of joy: "Bless ye the Lord, all His elect; keep days of joy and give glory to Him. Jerusalem, city of God, the Lord hath chastised thee for the work of thy hands. Give glory to the Lord for thy good things and bless the God eternal, that He may rebuild His tabernacle in thee and may call back all the captives to thee, and thou mayest rejoice for ever and ever. Nations from afar shall come to thee and shall bring gifts and shall adore the Lord in thee and shall esteem thy land as holy. For they shall call upon the great Name in thee. Blessed shall they be that shall build thee up! Blessed are all they that love thee and rejoice in thy peace!" (Tob. 10: 18.)

How are we to earn a share in this blessing? How may we add some stones to the spiritual temple of the Catholic Church in England? Let us never forget that on us English Catholics, and on us alone, rests the burden of responsibility. If we love our country, can her future be indifferent to us? Now that future depends under God upon ourselves.

The English people, so long separated from the truth and ignorant almost of its first principles, turn naturally to those who have been faithful to it or whom God's mercy has led back to it, to see what it is and what it does for its professors. What they see us to be, that they judge the Church to be. If we are fervent, charitable, devout, full of good works, mortified, self-sacrificing — in a word true children of the martyrs — they will be attracted irresistibly towards the faith which we profess. But if they find us lukewarm, indifferent, worldly, or worse, what will they think of the faith which we pretend to cherish, to uphold, and to set forth to men? Ah! My brethren, the indifferent lives of too many of us are the chiefest stumbling block in the way of England's conversion.

Not for our own sake alone, but for the sake of those millions who lie outside in darkness, let us show forth Christ in our lives,

> And preach the Faith as love knows how
> By kindly deeds and virtuous life.

Then we shall at least not have upon our hands the blood of our separated countrymen, the guilt of the loss of immortal souls.

And the martyrs encourage us to pray, and to pray earnestly for the consummation of their blessed work. How can we forget their tears, their blood which cries continually to God for England? Have we less love for her than those foreign Catholics who pray so perseveringly for her conversion? Let us each of us ask himself today: "Do I pray daily for the conversion of England?" And if not, let him begin today upon this feast of the martyrs. One *Hail Mary*, one *Jesus, convert England*, one aspiration to our martyrs will not overburden our devotions. But let us do more. Let us put this object continually before us. Let us pray for it constantly, night and day. Whenever we hear the clock strike, for instance, or whenever we see our Lord Jesus Christ lifted up in the hands of His priests at the sacring of the Holy Mass.

Let us pray, too, for individuals, that our prayers may be the more fervent. And let us pray with persevering faith, even though it be years before we are heard. Or again, we may pray especially for those nearest to the light or for those who are seeking it with a sincere heart, or for those whose time on earth is short. We may ask our Lord to give us one soul every day, and we may be sure that He will hear us — though it may not be the very soul we desire but another whom He sees is better prepared for the grace.

And to our prayers the martyrs teach us to join charity and sacrifice. We must get at men's hearts if we are to win them. We shall never win our countrymen by sarcasm or ridicule. This only closes hearts against us. Let us try rather to thank God for what is good in them and in the system in which they have been reared. We need a Christ-like love of souls; we need a persevering hopefulness that no difficulties can daunt. Remember that we have God on our side, and that God never forgets. "And Sion said: The Lord has forsaken me and the Lord has forgotten me. Can a woman forget her infant, so as not to have pity on the son of her womb? Well, if she should forget, yet will I not forget thee. Behold I have engraven thee in my hands, thy walls are always before my eyes." (Isaiah 49:14-16) Yes, we have cause to hope: through all those centuries of trial God had never forgotten us. And now he asks us to take our share in His work of restoring love.

And then there is sacrifice. No work is complete without the mark of the cross — the martyrs teach us that. Our Lord put prayer and fasting together as the necessary conditions for expelling demons, and we who wish to drive out from our land the demon of heresy dare not neglect this divine weapon. There have been souls who, inspired by the example of our martyrs, have risen to heroic acts of sacrifice for this great cause; generous souls who have offered their lives to God for the conversion of England, and whose sacrifice has been accepted. These are martyrs of charity, hidden from the world, indeed, but reigning with God amid the white-robed host, whose glory shall one day be proclaimed before men and angels. If we do not feel the call to heights such as this, let us at least offer to our God the sacrifice of mortified lives. Then, indeed, we may hope to gain some souls for Christ. Oh! what a joy for us if at the last great day, when the martyrs of England pass in glorious procession before the throne of God, singing their hymns of triumph and bearing their sheaves with them, if we — yes, even we — may follow in their steps and lay before the feet of our Redeemer but one soul whom we have rescued from eternal death!

Jesus, convert England! Jesus, have mercy on this country! Holy Mother Mary, have pity on thy dower!

VI

The Martyrs of York Champions of Christ

Tuesday, May 28, 1901, in Whitsunweek on the occasion of the
Ransom Pilgrimage

*"Introeat in conspectu tuo gemitus compeditorum: secundum
magnitudinem brachii Tui posside filios mortificatorum — Let
the sighing of the prisoners come in before thee: according to
the greatness of thine arm take possession of the children of
them that have been put to death." — Ps. 76:11*

You are, all of you, acquainted with the story of the
Maccabees. It was an awful crisis in the history of God's chosen
people: the most terrible crisis that they yet had known. The pagan
tyrant who subjugated and ravaged their country had determined
to make conquest not only of their bodies but of their souls.

The choice of apostasy or death was offered to the hapless
Jews; the swine's flesh was thrust into the reluctant lips of
thousands; they were forced to crown themselves with ivy in honor
of Bacchus, and to turn from the pure worship of the one true God
to the foul and impious rites of Jupiter and Venus. Worse than all,
the most holy temple of God was shamelessly and horribly polluted,
its sacred courts rang with licentious revelry, and hogs were
sacrificed on the very altar.

Yet in this time of darkness and horror there were some
bright spots to relieve the universal gloom. There were the brave
men who fled to the mountains with the noble Judas Machabeus,
and prepared to sell their lives dearly in defense of the faith; there
was the holy old priest Eleazar, who so steadfastly refused even to
simulate apostasy for the sake of the young men who looked up to

him as a counselor and an example; there was, above all, that heroic mother with her seven martyr sons.

Now, during the sixteenth century after Christ, this England of ours went through a crisis not less terrible and strangely parallel with that of Judea in the time of Antiochus Epiphanes. True, it was no foreign pagan who gained possession of our shores, but what alien conqueror could have worked such universal devastation, such irreparable wrong to this poor land as the Christian prince, once the support and pillar of the Church, the champion of orthodoxy, the defender of the faith, Henry VIII, with his ill-omened offspring, Edward and Elizabeth?

Had you passed through the land at the beginning of his reign what would you have seen from one end of the kingdom to the other, from holy Canterbury to lordly Durham? You would have seen splendid abbeys, churches, monasteries and shrines innumerable, from which the incense of prayer and supplication was wafted ceaselessly up to the throne of the Most High; in which the sacred offices of the Church were ever daily celebrated with a magnificence of detail and a pomp of ceremonial unsurpassed before or since in the history of the Church.

You might have passed from the glorious golden shrine of St. Thomas of Canterbury to the equally splendid tomb of the royal Confessor in his abbey at Westminster; and from thence to where St. Alban, the protomartyr, rested in sacred splendor on the hill of Verulam; or where the virgin Queen Etheldreda or the royal martyr Edmund cast a heavenly blessing over the fens of Cambridgeshire and the plains of East Anglia. But nowhere surely were shrines more stately or holy places more abundant than amid the hills and dales of this fair shire, never a city more sacred than this ancient and venerable metropolis, in whose defense St. Edwin shed his blood, and within whose circling walls St. William, as St. Paulinus and St. Wilfrid before him, set up his pastoral throne. And if I do not speak of Beverley and Ripon, of Selby and Fountains, of Rievaulx and Bolton, and a hundred more, it is because their very stones cry out — each an undying witness, like that mighty Minster under whose shadow we are gathered — of the faith and hope and charity of Yorkshiremen, their love for holy Church and their devotion to the See of Peter.

So it was in England, in Yorkshire, when Henry Tudor mounted his father's throne; and so it might yet be, had it not been for the unbridled passions of that unhappy prince. Like a bolt from the blue, upon all this prosperity and peace and splendor, came the fatal news of the king's apostasy, and the summons to follow and imitate him in his downward career. And those who bore the first brunt of the storm were those ancient houses of religion which the piety of our fathers had founded—the patrimony of St. Benedict, of St. Bernard, of St. Dominic and St. Francis. The greedy king, whose rapacity could not have been sated by rivers of gold, seized on these venerable shrines. One by one they fell, pillaged and stripped and destroyed piecemeal. Worse still, the relics of God's saints were scattered to the dust, and few were so happy as were St. William of York and St. John of Beverley, whose sacred dust was spared, while their rich shrines became the prey of the spoiler. Everywhere ruin and desolation, famine and pestilence, stalked through the land; the poor nuns lay down to die of hunger by the roadside; the monks were thrown into dungeons or exiled into foreign lands.

Nor was this the worst. Prelates, priests and people in large numbers were terrified or cajoled into submitting to the new religion, and worshipping the golden idol of the royal supremacy. It was a national apostasy.

But amid all this gloom, England had yet her Maccabees that noble Pilgrimage of Grace, with its heroic leader, Robert Aske, of Yorkshire, who rose here in the North Country in defense of the monasteries and the religion of their fathers. "For God, our Lady and the Catholic faith," their watchword, and the Five Wounds of our dear Lord their badge, they entered the city, and fixed a proclamation on the Minster door, inviting the ejected religious to return to their monasteries, and demanding the extirpation of heresy, and the restoration of the ancient supremacy of the Apostolic See. Unhappily they had to contend against a foe as crafty as he was bloodthirsty—they trusted to the delusive promises of the king, and disbanded, only to find themselves at the mercy of one who knew no mercy. And so through the streets of York, Robert Aske, the Judas Machabeus of England, was drawn as a traitor upon a hurdle, the first of the long line of sufferers who were to glorify this city by their blood.

England had, too, her Eleazar (and we, Yorkshiremen, may well be proud of him), a worthy representative indeed of the holy Jewish scribe, Blessed John Fisher, born in Beverley, as we love to remember, Cardinal of the holy Roman Church and Bishop of Rochester. He, like his protomartyr, stood up almost alone against the impious king, and won in his old age a martyr's crown, "leaving to the whole nation the memory of his death for an example of virtue and fortitude."

Yes, and England, too, saw the wonderful sight of a mother offering with gladness and thankful joy not alone her seven sons, but seven times seven to death and torments in the cause of God.

Yes, it is thou, O holy Church of York, bride of St. William, and faithful daughter of the Apostolic See, who in the days of darkness and sorrow didst rear thy sons for martyrdom, and didst behold, without flinching, no less than nine and forty of thy sons butchered before thine eyes. Thou art robed in the imperial purple of their sacred blood; more glorious now in thy desolation than in the days of old, when kings were thy nursing fathers and queens thy nursing mothers. God forbid that we, thy sons, should glory save in the cross of our Lord Jesus Christ!

We will glory in the sufferings and the constancy of our brethren, who in the evil day did not bow the knee to Baal; we will glory above all in those seven times seven sons of thy womb who counted not the cost but were glad to resist even unto blood!

They, by their fidelity, by their constancy in suffering, consoled the Sacred Heart of their Lord, for, as we are constantly reminded in Paschal-tide, *in servis suis consolabitur Deus*.[16] That was all the reward they asked, that they might give back love for love, and life for life; but God, who is never to be outdone in generosity, gave them in recompense an eternal crown, and exceeding weight of glory.

It is impossible in the brief time at our dispoal to speak in detail of these glorious martyrs but bear with me if I try to put

---

[16] In Servis Suis Consalabitur Deus - God shall find His consolation in His servants.

before you very briefly scenes from the lives of one or the other of them, so that you may at least desire to know more of them, and knowing them better, to walk more faithfully in their steps.

They were not all priests; there were indeed many laymen among that glorious band, gentlemen of high degree, and sturdy yeomen from the dales, besides one saintly woman, that fair and gentle matron, whom men call the "Pearl of York."[17] Indeed, it was no uncommon sight to see hanging together on the sacred gibbet at Knavesmire, the seminary priest who had taken his life in his hands to bring to his beloved country the message of the gospel and the healing strength of the sacraments, and beside him the humble layman, who had received him as an angel of God, had taken him into his house and sheltered and relieved him, and had thus, like Alban of old, received the reward of his hospitality.

The majority, perhaps, of these martyrs, and it is an encouragement for us Ransomers to remember that fact today, were converts to the Catholic faith. And truly wonderful are the stories of some of those conversions. There, for instance, was Henry Walpole, who, as a young man and a Protestant, stood at Tyburn among a crowd of curious spectators to see the martyrdom of Blessed Edmund Campion and his companions. And as he pressed near the scaffold, one drop of the martyr's blood darted forth from his quivering heart and fell on him. And the contact of that sacred blood transformed him in an instant, and won for him the grace of conversion to the true faith — yes, and of vocation to the Society of Jesus. And so, after labors manifold and torments unsurpassed (we read that he was racked full fourteen times), Henry Walpole is in his turn drawn to our Tyburn at York, there to receive the reward of his fidelity to grace.

Or take another example. It is a young Yorkshireman, rich and worldly, who is on his travels in foreign parts. He comes to Douay, where the famous Dr. Allen, afterwards Cardinal, has lately founded the celebrated English College. The young man, who is a bigoted Protestant, calls upon Allen in order to convert him from

---

[17] The "Pearl of York" refers to St. Margaret of Clitheroe.

his Romish errors to the new gospel. He is courteously received, and many an argument takes place between them; until at last the youth is put to silence and confusion. But he will not yield; on the contrary, if he cannot defend his faith in words he is willing to fight for it, and he announces to Dr. Allen that he is going to join the Protestants, who are in revolt in the Netherlands against the King of Spain. The good doctor, seeing that argument is useless, tells him that he will betake himself to prayer; and all that night he spends in fervent supplication for this strayed sheep of our Lord's fold. And lo! in the morning William Andleby comes back, and, throwing himself at Dr. Allen's feet, begs him in floods of tears to receive him into God's Church; for prayer has been heard, as faithful fervent prayer is ever heard, and grace has made its conquest of that noble, wayward heart. And in his turn William Andleby becomes a fervent priest, a self-sacrificing missionary, and after nearly twenty years spent in his own dear Yorkshire, amid unwearied labors and perpetual dangers, laid down at last his life for Christ at yonder Tyburn, and went to receive his crown.

But let us turn to the protomartyrs of our church of York, the eldest sons of this mother of martyrs, the Carthusians, Blessed James Walworth and John Rochester. Let us see how these holy monks prepared for death. When the apostate king demanded of the brethren of the London Charterhouse the oath which acknowledged him, in the place of Peter, to be supreme Head of the Church in England, the prior, Blessed John Houghton, called his brethren together in the Chapter, and bade them prepare to die. And after they had cleansed their souls in the sacrament of penance, these heroic men calmly prepared for their doom, not less beautiful in their resolution, says Froude, "not less deserving the everlasting remembrance of mankind than those 300 who, in the summer morning, sat combing their yellow hair in the passes of Thermopylae. Nor in this hour of trial were they left without higher comfort."[18]

---

[18] Froude, James A. (1818-1894) an English Historian. This quote is from *History of England Vol. II*, 1875.

They met on the morrow in the Chapter House, and after their holy prior had addressed to them a most moving exhortation, he prayed them to do as they saw him do. And then he went and knelt down before the feet of each of his sons, and humbly begged his forgiveness for any offence in thought, word or deed, which he might have committed against him. And so they all did each in his turn, craving mutual forgiveness with tears. And then in the church they sang a solemn votive Mass of the Holy Ghost. And we are told by one who was then present that during the Holy Sacrifice, God, the almighty and merciful, deigned to work wondrous and ineffable signs. For when the most Sacred Host was lifted up there thrilled through the choir a soft whisper of heavenly music, lighter than air, which filled their hearts with peace and consolation. The prior sank down at the altar bathed in tears, and the brethren knelt in a rapture of silent prayer, for they perceived with joy that God was indeed with them. It is well that today, in this octave of Pentecost, we should recall that wondrous Mass of the Holy Ghost when the great Paraclete, the Comforter, deigned thus tenderly to soothe the fears of the protomartyrs of the Reformation, and to nerve them for the conflict before them. Eighteen of them are now numbered among the blessed, and two of those gained their crowns at York.

Here, after innumerable hardships, they were hanged in chains, and their sacred bodies long remained on the gallows, a sight terrible indeed to men, but unspeakably dear to the angels of God.

Nor did our martyrs shrink from the conflict. Witness that aged man who, arrested by a foul traitor near Thirsk, was carried off to York. Burdened by the weight of 87 years and cruel infirmities he could not sit upon horseback, and his captor was obliged to fling him across the animal's back. Thus they journeyed. By easy stages, etc., he brought him to York, where their passage through the streets was long remembered and spoken of by the other inhabitants with indignation and horror. When at last they reached the castle, the traitor, having delivered up his prisoner, was about to ride off. "Hark you, Cuthbert," said the old man, "I have ever given you a great deal of trouble in bringing me to this happy

WITNESSES TO THE HOLY MASS

place, here take this coin for your pains, and the Lord be with you!"

And when he was dragged together with a young priest to the place of execution, he insisted on mounting first the fatal ladder, in order to encourage his young companion. But finding it a hard task, he had to halt on his way up, and he turned to the sheriff and said, with a smile, "Good Mr. Sheriff, have a little patience with me; indeed this same climbing a ladder is a piece of hard service for an old man of fourscore years and seven; however, I will do my best, for who would not take thus much pains to get heaven at the journey's end? And so the Venerable John Lockwood passed to his reward.

But this joyous calm at the last hour was sometimes won by a cruel conflict with the powers of darkness. Witness the holy martyr, Alexander Crow, who from being a poor shoemaker in this city, was advanced by God's mercy to the dignity of the priesthood.

The night before his death, as he lay in York Castle, he had to undergo a terrible struggle with the enemy of souls, who appeared to him under a terrifying aspect, assuring him that his soul was lost, and trying to drive him to despair and suicide. A trembling fellow-prisoner was a witness of his agony, and has preserved the story for us. At last, after half an hour of conflict, he saw a great light come in at the door, and there appeared to him the blessed forms of our dear Lady and St. John, who put the demon to flight, saying, "Begone from hence, thou cursed creature; thou hast no part in this servant of Christ, who will shed his blood tomorrow for his Lord, and will enter into His joy."

I need not remind you of her who went so sweetly to her awful doom, giving alms as was her wont, and saying, "This way to heaven is as short as any other." The Catholics of York will never forget her, and she has made Ousebridge as dear to us and sacred as the Tyburn at Knavesmire.[19]

Such were the martyrs of York — the children whom this venerable mother offered to God through the long night of her sorrow.

---

[19] St. Margaret Clitheroe

But they were only the leaders—who shall speak of the uncounted multitudes of faithful souls who followed them, who animated by their words and example resisted if not unto blood, at least till death, after weary years in fetid dungeon and dreary prison house? Only when the secrets of all hearts are revealed will the Church of York bring forth her hidden treasures to the admiring gaze of angels and men. Yet we know enough of them to know that on the last day there will rise from beneath the shadow of the Castle walls, from Toft Green, and from unnumbered graves from every churchyard of this city, the bodies of hundreds, nay thousands, who suffered a lifelong agony for the Holy Faith.

There will be those simple souls, so dear to God, whose testimony against the new religion has come down to us, inscribed by their persecutors on the records of this city. Old men and maidens, young men and widows, when haled before their judges they had but one reply. They would not go to the church; they would not join in the heretical worship of the new religion — because there was neither priest, nor altar, nor sacrifice, and their conscience would not allow them. They would remain, they protested, in the faith in which they had been baptized. Precious is their testimony to us against the sophistries of those who in our own day would gladly claim for themselves and for their newfangled creed the inalienable and sacred name of Catholic! Against such pretensions there arise an exceedingly large cloud of witnesses from this venerable city, men and women of high and low degree who were content to rot in the loathsome dungeons of the Kidcote or the castle rather than to purchase life and liberty by one act of communion with heretics. Their names are written in the Book of Life, and their souls like precious jewels rest on the heart of God.

"Let the sighing of the prisoners come in before Thee! according to the greatness of Thine arm take possession of the children of those who have been put to death!" (Ps. 78: 11)

What are we to learn today from the martyrs of York? Surely first and above all things to value more deeply, and cling to more faithfully, and love more passionately that Holy Faith to which they witnessed and for which they died. We have entered into their heritage, and enjoy the fruit of their labors and their blood. We

WITNESSES TO THE HOLY MASS

owe them a debt that only God can estimate, as only God can pay.
But at least we owe them, do we not, a steadfast and unflinching
loyalty to holy Church and to that Apostolic See for whose rights
they shed their blood? It was their chief glory and their boast. Oh!
Let it be ours! To be children of the holy Church! Oh, gracious
Lord, we pray "take possession of the children of them that have
been put to death"; take possession of us, our hearts and our wills!
Adveniat regnum tuum![20] Mayest Thou ever rule in our hearts as
our supreme Lord and Master; let faith be the light of our lives,
and Thy love the motive of our every action. Then, and only then,
will dawn the longed-for day of England's final conversion. Yes,
the martyrs teach us that we must begin with ourselves. We are
banded together in work and prayer for the conversion of England,
for that most blessed end for which these martyrs sighed and toiled
and shed their blood. "Take Thou possession, O Lord," we cry,
"of the children of those who have been put to death." Look upon
the sighing of the prisoners, on those countless souls so dear to us
who lie enchained in the bondage of error, in the prison houses of
Thine enemy. We would gladly ransom them, would we not? It is
for that end that we have come together today to this holy city of
the martyrs, to offer the dread oblation and invoke the intercession
of the saints. But if we would free them, let us first be sure that we
are not ourselves bond slaves to any evil passion or unregulated
affection. Let us rejoice in the liberty of the sons of God; it is
Christ who makes us free. We have some of us known what it is to
groan in the darkness and to stretch our weary hands to the light
we could not see. And God, in answer, we doubt not, to the ceaseless
intercession of His martyrs, has had pity on our misery, and opened
the door of our prison house, and "brought us out of the mire and
clay and set our feet upon a rock—yea, upon *The Rock*—and
ordered our goings. And He has put a new song into our mouths,
even a thanksgiving unto our God." And He has filled our souls
with a quenchless longing for those we have left behind, for those
dear, upright, pure souls who are so far more worthy of His grace

---

[20] Adveniat regnum tuum - Thy Kingdom Come

than we were, and whom we would give our lives to win. And so we pray, and we make pilgrimage, and we look with hope to the saints and martyrs of England to hear and answer us speedily.

Yet, in many cases, we seem to plead in vain! Is it, perhaps, sometimes that we have not yet given ourselves up with wholehearted, ungrudging generosity to the call of God, that we have fallen so grievously short of the martyr standard, that we have shrunk so weakly from the cross and the conflict within? If it be so with one or other of you, let him beg for strength from the dear martyrs today. Let him ask that valiant woman, whose relics we shall venerate, to obtain for him a courage that will never flinch from self-sacrifice, and a faith that will vanquish every obstacle. Let us ask it, each of us, as we kneel at St. William's grave, and at the place of martyrdom, for a greater share of the spirit of the saints, a greater love for the cross, a deeper insight into the mysteries of our most holy religion.

England will not be converted till we have saints among us once more. My brethren, let us ask for saints! Raise up, O Lord, among us the spirit of those unvanquished martyrs of Thine, who here poured out their blood for Thee. "Take possession, we beseech Thee, of the children of them that have been put to death!"